T
O
K

Y

FOR MY PARENTS,
SATORU AND MARIKO MUROTA

MAORI MUROTA

Tokyo

CULT RECIPES

PHOTOGRAPHS BY AKIKO IDA AND PIERRE JAVELLE
STYLING BY MAORI MUROTA AND SABRINA FAUDA-ROLE
GRAPHIC DESIGN AND ILLUSTRATIONS BY PLAYGROUND PARIS
ILLUSTRATED NOTES BY MAORI MUROTA

HARPER
DESIGN
An Imprint of HarperCollinsPublishers

昔ながらの
ラーメン
ramen soup topped with
slices of roasted pork
750円

昔ながらの
チャーシューメン
ramen soup topped with
slices of roasted pork
1000円

肉うどん
hot soup udon with beef
900円

カレー
うどん
hot soup udon with curry
800円

天ぷらそば
hot soup soba with tempura
250円

天ぷらうどん
hot soup udon with tempura
1250円

しらす月見そば
hot soup soba with young of the
sardine and raw egg
900円

梅おろしそば
hot soup soba with a pickled
ume
850円

hot soup soba with raw egg and grated yam

シンプルに
あんみつ
650円

白玉あんみつ
shiratama anmitsu
もちもちの白玉
700円

白玉クリーム
あんみつ
shiratama cream anmitsu
当店おすすめ
800円

クリーム
あんみつ
cream anmitsu
750円

当店の甘味にはすべて
お抹茶が付いております。
京都宇治産・堀田勘兵衛商店の抹茶使用

抹茶はふぇ
matcha parfait
90

豆かん
700

抹茶ぜんざい
matcha zenzai
甘さ控えめ・あたたかい
700円

ぜんざい
zenzai
北海道大納言使用
650円

冷やし
大納言ぜんざい
cold daingyon zenzai
700円

甘酒セット

紅葉
白米の甘酒

お抹茶セット

冷やし抹茶
クリームぜんざい

Tokyo

CONTENTS

PREFACE
はじめに

When I arrived in France, I noticed that Japanese food wasn't very well understood there. It was often confused with other Asian cuisines, or else it had a fairly limited image. People would ask me: **"So, do you eat sushi every day at home?"** No, not all that often. It is more of a special occasion meal orchestrated by a sushi master at a restaurant. **"I don't like tofu, it's bland."** There are many ways of preparing tofu, and it is also important to choose the right tofu for each dish. **"Miso soup has no flavor. It's just salty."** Make your miso soup with real dashi stock, and you are sure to change your mind! So I started giving cooking classes. Not just for sushi and yakitori, but also for the everyday dishes eaten in Japan. What a pleasure to hear the responses: **"Japanese cooking is so simple!** There are a lot of flavors I didn't know about. What looked complicated isn't that hard!" **Yes, it is simple.** You just need to learn a few basic techniques and how to identify and use quality ingredients. Becoming a sushi master may not be within everyone's reach, but everyday Japanese cooking is not difficult to learn. Born in Tokyo, I grew up there with parents who were passionate about food. My father, a real Tokyoite and proud of it, took me to all the restaurants he loved, from luxurious sushi restaurants at one end of the scale to *yatai*, the crude but incredibly good mobile yakitori stands at the other, with traditional soba noodle restaurants in the Asakusa district in between. My mother, equally enthusiastic about food, made a bento box for me every day to take to school. Or rather, she made the best bento of the class, the one everyone wanted to taste. **At home we cooked together, and every meal was a topic of serious discussion!** So, in this book, I want to introduce you to the authentic dishes of the Tokyo I grew up in—the food cooked at home and the food served in restaurants. The recipes are drawn from my memory and the trip I made for this book, visiting my favorite neighborhoods and going back to family sources. I hope this book will help you discover the true flavors of Tokyo and Japan. **I will be delighted if it inspires your everyday cooking and gives you the pleasure of sharing it with someone!**

Maori

室田　万央里

OPPOSITE:
MY MOTHER'S RECIPE NOTEBOOK,
STARTED WHEN I WAS BORN.

朝定食

ASA TEISHOKU

BREAKFAST

The traditional Japanese breakfast is made up of rice, miso soup, tsukemono (pickles), fish and eggs. This meal is an integral part of Japanese cuisine because it contains the essential elements of our dishes, such as rice and dashi (stock). In day-to-day life, we don't always have time to make this traditional breakfast, instead having coffee, toast and pancakes in the Western style, but it is still very much enjoyed.

米の炊き方 PREPARING RICE

RICE PORTION SIZES

SERVES 4
300 g (12¾ oz), or 2 gō, of Japanese white rice
430 ml (15 fl oz/1¾ cups) water

The gō is a Japanese unit of measurement: 1 gō equals 150 g (5½ oz) or 180 ml (6 fl oz) of rice. The amount needed for a bowl of rice for 1 person is 75 g (2¾ oz), or 90 ml (3 fl oz), so 1 gō is the ideal quantity for 2 people. To make this step easier, find a glass that holds 1 gō—you'll need 1⅛ glasses of water for each glass of rice. The weight of rice increases by 2.5 times when cooked, thus 75 g (2¾ oz) rice becomes about 190 g (6¾ oz).

PREPARATION

35 MINS PREPARATION TIME—**18 MINS** COOKING TIME

1. Washing
Place the rice in a large bowl. Pour in some water and mix with your hands, then immediately discard the water (use a strainer to drain the rice). Next, "sharpen" the rice. This is the Japanese term for removing the excess starch by washing the grains. Cup your hand as if you were holding a baseball. Plunge your cupped hand into the rice and turn it about 20 times, tracing small circles. Pour some more water into the bowl; it will turn cloudy. Discard this water immediately and "sharpen" the rice again. Pour in some water and discard. Repeat this process 3 to 4 times until the water in the bowl is clear.

2. Draining
Drain the rice in a strainer and let it rest for 30 minutes.

3. Soaking in water
Place the rice in a heavy-based saucepan (or a flameproof casserole dish) with a lid, so the rice doesn't burn. Pour in the required amount of water. Let the rice soak briefly so it absorbs some water before cooking.

4. Cooking
Cover the saucepan and bring to a boil on medium heat (about 5 minutes). Lower the heat to the minimum setting and cook for about 12–13 minutes (avoid removing the lid after reducing the heat). Take the pan off the heat and let the rice rest for 10 minutes. This ensures that the rice swells up properly. Remove the lid and use a spatula to stir the rice, going right to the bottom of the pan without mashing the grains—if the grains stick, wet the spatula.

TIPS

If you want to buy a rice cooker, choose a Japanese model if you can afford it, because Chinese rice cookers are generally designed to cook Chinese rice, which has lower levels of starch and water. If you are short on time, you can skip steps 2 and 3 (although the rice won't be as good), but never skip step 1 or the excess starch and any unpleasant taint won't be properly removed.

Rice is an essential food for the Japanese. Not just a side dish, rice is as important as the rest of the meal. More than 300 varieties are grown, but those that are short-grained and high in starch are preferred. Japanese consumers take their choice of brand seriously and are prepared to spend money on expensive rice cookers to get the best results. For the Japanese, cooking the right rice perfectly is a passion.

These are the quantities of cooked rice to prepare according to the dish:

For 1 small bowl of rice to serve with
  a standard dish: 150 g (5½ oz)
For 1 large bowl of rice for donburi
  (various toppings on a bed of rice): 280 g (10 oz)
For 1 sushi: 18 g (¾ oz)
For 1 large onigiri: 100 g (3½ oz)
  For a small one: 60 g (2¼ oz)

For example, to make a donburi dish for 4 people, you will need about 1.1 kg (2 lb 7 oz) cooked rice. This corresponds to 450 g (1 lb) uncooked rice.

01

02

03

出汁 D A S H I

OI

Dashi is the essential base stock of Japanese cuisine. It is used in particular to make miso soup, in combination with miso paste. The most common ingredients of dashi are water, katsuobushi (dried bonito flakes) and kombu (dried seaweed). Unfortunately, many Japanese people today no longer make their own dashi but use instant powdered or liquid substitutes for speed and convenience. Instant dashi, however, often contains amino acids and glutamates that flatten the flavor of dishes, which I think is a real shame. Just once, I recommend you make dashi yourself. It is a little expensive and it takes time, but its incomparable flavor is well worth the effort! With practice, the technique becomes second nature and you can easily make dashi while preparing other dishes.

TIPS

You can freeze dashi in resealable freezer bags or ice-cube trays and take out the amount you need whenever you want. Make sure you seal the package of bonito shavings well after opening because it easily absorbs humidity and odors.
If you use instant dashi, try to find one without amino acids or glutamates. Dilute with water according to the quantities indicated on the package.

INGREDIENTS AND QUANTITIES

1 liter (35 fl oz/4 cups) water
10 g (¼ oz) kombu seaweed
10 g (¼ oz) katsuobushi (dried bonito flakes)

It is easy to remember the quantities of katsuobushi and kombu: 1% of the quantity of water.

PREPARATION

40 MINS PREPARATION TIME—**17 MINS** COOKING TIME

1. Soaking in water
Place the water in a saucepan. Cut the kombu into 2 pieces and add to the water, then leave to soak for at least 30 minutes in the refrigerator. You can do this the night before or a few hours ahead of time.

2. Cooking the dashi
Heat the water on low heat until it just comes to a simmer, about 15 minutes. Don't let it boil, or the seaweed flavor will be too strong. Take out the kombu just before the stock comes to a boil and add the katsuobushi all at once. Bring to a boil on medium heat, then turn off the heat immediately. Let it infuse for 10 minutes.

3. Straining
Strain the dashi into a bowl. Let the dashi drip through, pressing lightly.

THE DIFFERENT TYPES OF MISO
味噌

One of the fundamental ingredients of Japanese cooking, miso is made from cooked soy beans and often rice or wheat (depending on the region), to which a fermentation agent is added. High in vitamin B and protein, it is believed to have anticarcinogenic properties. Used to make miso soup, an almost indispensable component of Japanese meals, it is also used as a condiment, in marinades for fish or meat, in sauces and even in desserts. Its color varies, according to the ingredients and the degree of fermentation. Misos can be roughly classified into three colors: red miso (aka-miso), brown miso (tanshoku-miso) and white miso (shiro-miso). You can combine several different misos to obtain the flavor you want, depending on the other ingredients in your dish, but I suggest you taste each miso by itself first.

BROWN MISO
淡色味噌

This miso is made from barley and soy beans (or rice and soy beans in the south of Japan). Its neutral flavor works well in soups with all kinds of ingredients, especially vegetables, tofu and seaweed. This is the most commonly used miso for everyday cooking, and when people refer to "miso" in Japan, this is generally the one they mean.

WHITE MISO
白味噌

This is a young miso that contains less salt and its fermentation time is quite short. It has a sweet and mild flavor. In soup, it works well with root vegetables and winter vegetables or pork. Meat is only very rarely added to miso soup, but an exception is made for pork. Since this miso is very mild-tasting, it is good to add some shichimi (7-spice mix), ginger or a little citrus zest to lift the flavor.

RED MISO
赤みそ

The taste of red miso is stronger than brown or white miso and its fermentation time is longer. In soup, it is often combined with strongly flavored seafood and vegetables, shiso (perilla) or grilled vegetables.

BROWN MISO # WHITE MISO # RED MISO

BROWN MISO + TOFU + WAKAME

BROWN MISO + PUMPKIN + ONION

BROWN MISO + ABURA-AGE + SHIITAKE

WHITE MISO + DAIKON (WHITE RADISH)

WHITE MISO + LOTUS ROOT + PORK

WHITE MISO + CHINESE CABBAGE

RED MISO + PRAWN + CHIVE

RED MISO + LEEK

RED MISO + OKRA + SHISO

+BROWN MISO

Base
600 ml (21 fl oz) dashi (see p. 12)
4 tablespoons brown miso

TOFU AND WAKAME

100 g (3½ oz) silken tofu
4 g (⅛ oz) wakame seaweed
Cut the tofu into 1 cm (½ in) cubes. Soak the wakame in a bowl of water for 5 minutes. Drain and cut into 2 cm (¾ in) lengths. Bring the dashi to a boil on high heat, then add the tofu and cook on medium-low heat for 1 minute. Add the wakame and stir the miso into the soup. Remove from the heat and serve.

PUMPKIN AND ONION

¼ onion
100 g (3½ oz) pumpkin
Cut the onion into 5 mm (¼ in) slices. Peel and seed the pumpkin. Cut into 5 mm (¼ in) slices and then into pieces about 3 cm x 2 cm (1¼ x ¾ in). Bring the dashi to a boil, then add the onion and pumpkin and cook on medium heat for 5 minutes. Stir the miso into the soup, remove from the heat and serve.

ABURA-AGE AND SHIITAKE

25 g (1 oz) abura-age
    (fried tofu sheets)
2 shiitake mushrooms
Cut the abura-age in half lengthwise, then into 1 cm (½ in) strips. Remove the stalks from the mushrooms, then cut the caps into 5 mm (¼ in) slices. Bring the dashi to a boil, then add the abura-age and mushrooms and cook on medium heat for 2 minutes. Stir the miso into the soup. Remove from the heat and serve.

+WHITE MISO

Base
600 ml (21 fl oz) dashi (see p. 12)
4 tablespoons white miso

DAIKON (WHITE RADISH)

4 cm (1½ in) daikon (white radish)
Slice the radish into 3 mm (⅛ in) rounds, then into thin matchsticks. Bring the dashi to a boil, add the radish and cook on medium heat for 3 minutes. Stir in the miso, remove from the heat and serve.

LOTUS ROOT AND PORK

3 cm (1¼ in) lotus root
70 g (2½ oz) thinly sliced
    pork neck or belly
1 teaspoon toasted sesame oil
shichimi (Japanese 7-spice mix)
Peel the lotus root and slice into 3 mm (⅛ in) rounds, then cut each round in half. Cut the slices of pork into thin strips about 2 cm (¾ in) wide. Heat the sesame oil in a saucepan on medium heat and sauté the pork until browned. Add the lotus root and continue to cook for 1 minute, then add the dashi. When it comes to a boil, lower the heat to medium-low and cook for 3 minutes. Stir in the miso, remove from the heat and serve. Sprinkle with shichimi.

CHINESE CABBAGE

3 leaves Chinese cabbage
1 cm (½ in) ginger
Cut each cabbage leaf into 3 pieces, and then into 6 mm (¼ in) strips. Cut the ginger into thin matchsticks. Bring the dashi to a boil, add the cabbage and cook on medium heat for 5 minutes. Add the ginger, then stir in the miso and serve.

+RED MISO

Base
600 ml (21 fl oz) dashi (see p. 12)
3 tablespoons red miso

PRAWN AND CHIVE

8 large raw prawns (shrimp),
    or cooked ones
2 chives, very finely chopped
Bring the dashi to a boil, then add the prawns and cook on medium heat for 5 minutes (or 3 minutes, if you are using cooked prawns). Skim off any foam, then stir in the miso, remove from the heat and serve. Sprinkle with chives.

LEEK

2 leeks, white parts only
2 tablespoons toasted sesame oil
2 chives, chopped
Cut the leeks into 2 cm (¾ in) lengths. Heat the oil in a saucepan on high heat and cook the leeks until the sides in contact with the saucepan have browned. Add the dashi and cook for 5 minutes on medium heat. Stir in the miso, then remove from the heat and serve. Sprinkle with the chives.

OKRA AND SHISO

5 okra
2 shiso (perilla) leaves,
    very finely shredded
Cut the okra into 3 mm (⅛ in) slices. Bring the dashi to a boil, then add the okra and cook on medium heat for about 1 minute. Stir in the miso, then remove from the heat and serve. Sprinkle with the shiso.

TSUKEMONO
JAPANESE PICKLES
漬け物

CHINESE CABBAGE

白菜の漬け物

SERVES 4
10 MINS PREPARATION TIME
2 HRS RESTING TIME

¼ Chinese cabbage
4 cm (1½ in) kombu seaweed
2–3 cm (¾–1¼ in) ginger
½ organic lemon
2 teaspoons coarse salt
1 teaspoon soy sauce

Cut the cabbage crosswise into 3, then lengthwise into 4 cm (1½ in) pieces. Cut the kombu into 2 cm (¾ in) squares. Peel and slice the ginger very thinly. Cut the zest of the lemon into very thin strips and squeeze its juice. Place everything in a resealable bag and eliminate any air. Seal the bag and massage it from the outside. Leave in the refrigerator for at least 2 hours before serving. The tsukemono can be stored for 2 days in the refrigerator.

TURNIP

蕪の漬け物

SERVES 4
5 MINS PREPARATION TIME
2 HRS RESTING TIME

2–3 very fresh turnips
3 cm (1¼ in) kombu seaweed, cut into small pieces

Pickling liquid
5 tablespoons rice vinegar
1 tablespoon raw (demerara) sugar
1 teaspoon coarse salt

Slice the turnips into very thin rounds, about 1–2 mm (1⁄16 in) thick (a mandoline works well). Set them aside in a bowl. Place the pickling liquid ingredients in a small saucepan on low heat and stir to dissolve the sugar and salt. Turn off the heat, then add the kombu. Pour the pickling liquid over the turnips in the bowl and mix well. Marinate for at least 2 hours. You can keep the tsukemono for 4 days in the refrigerator.

CUCUMBER AND CARROT

キュウリと人参の漬け物

SERVES 4
20 MINS PREPARATION TIME
2 HRS RESTING TIME

½ cucumber
1 teaspoon coarse salt
1 carrot

Pickling liquid
3 tablespoons soy sauce
3 tablespoons rice vinegar
1 teaspoon sugar
1 garlic clove, crushed
1 cm (½ in) ginger, finely chopped

Cut the cucumber into bite-size triangular chunks and place in a bowl. Combine with the salt and leave for 10 minutes to draw out the liquid. Cut the carrot into similar-size pieces and add to the bowl. Combine the pickling liquid ingredients in a glass or ceramic container, then add the cucumber and carrot. Set aside in the refrigerator for at least 2 hours, stirring from time to time. You can keep the tsukemono for 2 days in the refrigerator.

卵焼き TAMAGO YAKI
ROLLED OMELETTE

SERVES 4

5 MINS PREPARATION TIME

5 MINS COOKING TIME

3 eggs
1 tablespoon dashi (see p. 12)
1 rounded tablespoon raw (demerara) sugar
1 teaspoon soy sauce
sunflower oil, for frying

Break the eggs into a bowl. Add the dashi, sugar and soy sauce and combine well. Heat a little oil in a medium-sized frying pan (about 22 cm/8½ in diameter). Remove any excess oil with a paper towel, making sure the whole surface of the frying pan is evenly coated with oil.

Pour in a fifth of the beaten egg mixture and spread it out very thinly, as for a crêpe. Before the surface is completely dry, roll the omelette toward the edge of the frying pan.

Pour in another fifth of the mixture and spread it out under the first roll. When it is cooked (without being dry), roll the new crêpe around the first roll. Repeat this process until you have used up all of the mixture.

Using a bamboo sushi mat, shape the omelette into an attractive square roll. Let it cool inside the mat. Slice the omelette roll into 6 pieces and serve.

01

03

04

02

05

ONSEN TAMAGO
JAPANESE SOFT-BOILED EGGS
温泉卵

SERVES 4

5 MINS PREPARATION TIME + OVERNIGHT RESTING TIME
18 MINS COOKING TIME

4 eggs, at room temperature

Dashi shoyu*
200 ml (7 fl oz) soy sauce
3 rounded tablespoons katsuobushi**
3 cm x 3 cm (1¼ in x 1¼ in) piece kombu seaweed

Place all of the dashi shoyu ingredients in a jar and let them
infuse overnight. If you don't have time, you can bring the mixture
to a boil in a saucepan, turn off the heat and let it infuse for
30 minutes. Dashi shoyu is a useful condiment for sashimi and
salads and as a substitute for soy sauce. As it will keep for 1 month
in the refrigerator, I recommend having some on hand all the time,
ready to use. Place the eggs in a small, heavy pot or casserole dish
with a well-fitting lid. Pour enough boiling water over to completely
cover the eggs. Cover with a lid and leave for 18 minutes.

Break an egg into each individual bowl and pour a tablespoon
of dashi shoyu over it.

** KATSUOBUSHI
= Dried bonito flakes

* DASHI SHOYU
出汁 醤油
kombu   katsuobushi
        soy
        sauce
Soy sauce flavored with
kombu and katsuobushi

NATTO
FERMENTED SOY BEANS
納豆

SERVES 1

5 MINS PREPARATION TIME

50 g (1¾ oz) package natto*
1 cm (½ in) slice of leek (white part), finely chopped
1 tablespoon soy sauce
1 very fresh egg
½ teaspoon Japanese mustard—optional

Place all the ingredients in a bowl. Whisk well with chopsticks to create a frothy texture. Serve in a small bowl accompanied by rice. To eat, pour the natto mixture over the rice. It has a very distinctive texture (slimy) and smell, but this is the must-have dish in the traditional Japanese breakfast.

* Natto is fermented soy beans. Often sold in individual packages, the most traditional kind is sold in a straw package, in which the beans have usually been fermented.

SALTED SALMON
塩鮭

SERVES 4

5 MINS PREPARATION TIME + AT LEAST **2 HRS** RESTING TIME
10 MINS COOKING TIME

4 salmon fillets—organic, if possible
4 teaspoons natural, unrefined coarse salt
3 cm (1¼ in) piece white radish (daikon), grated

Rub both sides of the salmon fillets with salt. Wrap in plastic wrap and leave to marinate for at least 2 hours, ideally overnight. Unwrap the salmon fillets and wipe dry. Preheat the oven to 200°C (400°F). Place the salmon in a baking dish and bake for about 10 minutes, depending on the size of the fillets. Serve the salted salmon with the grated radish.

SHISO LEAVES
FRESH TOFU WITH TWO SAUCES (OPPOSITE)

豆腐 TOFU

Tofu is a bean curd made from curdled soy milk, often presented in the form of a block, with a relatively neutral and subtle flavor.

PRODUCTION

Artisan producers make tofu very early in the morning, so they can sell it at breakfast time. They start by making the soy milk: the soy beans are soaked overnight, crushed and mixed with water. The liquid is filtered through a cloth, producing the soy milk and the soy pulp, called "okara." To make the tofu, a salty or sour coagulating agent is added to the soy milk to curdle it. Traditionally, nigari (magnesium chloride), a sea salt extract, is used. The whey is then removed before the curds are pressed in a mold.

VARIETIES

There are two main types of tofu. Silken tofu (kinugoshi dofu) is soft, smooth as silk and has a high water content. It is eaten uncooked (with soy sauce in hiyayakko) or in miso soup. Firm tofu (momen dofu) is denser and is stir-fried with meat, deep-fried and dipped in dashi (agedashi dofu), simmered in hot pots or mashed and fried like meatballs (ganmodoki).

HIYAYAKKO
FRESH TOFU WITH TWO SAUCES
冷や奴

** SHICHIMI
= 七味
Japanese 7-spice mix

mandarin zest
sesame seeds
hemp seeds
sansho pepper
poppy seeds
red chili
aonori

CUCUMBER–SHICHIMI SAUCE
SERVES 4
IO MINS PREPARATION TIME

300 g (10½ oz) block silken tofu*
½ cucumber + 1 pinch salt
3 cm (1¼ in) slice of leek (white part)
1 cm (½ in) ginger, peeled
2 teaspoons unrefined fine salt
1 tablespoon fish sauce
1 teaspoon raw (demerara) sugar
3 tablespoons toasted sesame oil
2 tablespoons rice vinegar
1 pinch shichimi**

Cut the block of tofu into 4 pieces. Dice the cucumber into 5 mm (¼ in) cubes. Mix with a pinch of salt and leave to rest for 5 minutes, then gently squeeze out the liquid with your hands. Finely chop the leek and ginger. In a small bowl, combine the cucumber, leek and ginger with the rest of the ingredients. Place the pieces of tofu in individual bowls and spoon over 1 heaped tablespoon of sauce just before serving.

KATSUO–SHISO SAUCE
SERVES 4
IO MINS PREPARATION TIME

300 g (10½ oz) block silken tofu*
2 shiso (perilla) leaves***
4 pinches katsuobushi (dried bonito flakes)
4 tablespoons soy sauce

Cut the block of tofu into 4 pieces. Shred the shiso leaves very finely. Place the pieces of tofu on individual plates and sprinkle over the shiso and katsuobushi. Spoon 1 tablespoon of soy sauce over each piece of tofu just before serving.

Note: The texture of the tofu is very important for this dish. It is best to use silken tofu, which contains more water and which you can find in organic food stores. Be careful—there are other tofus that are much firmer and denser than silken tofu. You can also use Chinese tofu if there isn't a Japanese food store close to you. Because tofu contains a lot of water, it will start to dilute the sauce as soon as you add it, so it is best to add the sauce at the last minute.

* SILKEN TOFU
= 絹豆腐
it contains a lot of water and is very smooth

*** SHISO
紫蘇
A very popular herb in Japan

TOFU SHOP IN THE NEZU DISTRICT
FRIED TOFU SHEETS (OPPOSITE)

飛竜頭(百合根)
200円

築地市場

TSUKIJI MARKET

Tokyo's Tsukiji Market is the largest fish market in the world, even if it is not exclusively devoted to seafood. The covered market (Jyounai), open every day, is reserved for trade customers until 9 am, but individuals can visit the outside market (Jyougai) from 5 am. The restaurants inside the market open very early for workers. They are known for their very fresh and inexpensive sushi, which attracts lots of tourists.

O H

I R

U

お昼

OHIRU

LUNCH

For lunch, we eat dishes that are simple to make and quick to eat. Noodles, rice, fish and meat are the essential ingredients of the meals carried in bento boxes (see p. 77) or served in restaurants. **Donburi**: different toppings on a bed of rice. **Soba**: buckwheat noodles stir-fried or cooked in a broth. The color of the broth varies from the north to the south of Japan. My mother, who is from the island of Kyushu, makes a very light broth. Growing up in Tokyo, I was shocked when I ate udon in a restaurant for the first time to see the noodles disappear into a black broth!

ZARU SOBA
BUCKWHEAT NOODLES AND SAUCE
ざる蕎麦

SERVES 4
10 MINS PREPARATION TIME
30 MINS COOKING TIME

Mentsuyu*
400 ml (14 fl oz) water
150 ml (5 fl oz) mirin
200 ml (7 fl oz) soy sauce
1 teaspoon raw
   (demerara) sugar
1 handful katsuobushi
   (dried bonito flakes)
5 cm x 5 cm (2 in x 2 in) piece
   kombu seaweed

350–400 g (12–14 oz)
   soba noodles
½ sheet nori, cut
   into thin strips
3 cm (1¼ in) white radish
   (daikon), peeled and grated
3 cm (1¼ in) ginger, peeled
   and grated
1 chive or 3 cm (1¼ in) leek
   (white part), very finely
   chopped
wasabi

To make the mentsuyu, place all the ingredients in a saucepan and cook on low heat for 20 minutes. Remove from the heat. You can keep the mentsuyu for 2 weeks in the refrigerator. I recommend that you double the recipe to use in the sōmen sauce recipe (see p. 244) or to make a hot broth for udon and soba noodles by diluting it with some dashi.

Cook the soba noodles according to the instructions on the package. Drain the noodles in a strainer, then run them under cold water for at least 20 seconds, swirling with your hands to remove the starch. Drain them well again.

Divide the noodles between woven bamboo baskets (zaru) or individual plates and top with the nori strips. Pour the mentsuyu into small bowls and dlute with some water, if you like. Serve with the radish, ginger, chive and wasabi on the side. Dip the ends of the soba noodles into the mentsuyu and enjoy.

* MENTSUYU
麺つゆ = sauce for
   noodles

Dip the ends
of the noodles

KAMO SOBA
BUCKWHEAT NOODLE SOUP WITH DUCK
鴨蕎麦

SERVES 4

10 MINS PREPARATION TIME

25 MINS COOKING TIME

300 g (10½ oz) duck breast
2 leeks (white part)
2 teaspoons vegetable oil

Soup
1.2 liters (42 fl oz) dashi (see p. 12)
5 tablespoons soy sauce
5 tablespoons mirin
350–400 g (12–14 oz) soba noodles
5 cm (2 in) white radish (daikon),
  or ½ black radish, peeled and grated
4 pieces yuzu zest*

Cut the duck breast into 6 mm (¼ in) slices and the leeks into 3 cm (1¼ in) lengths. Heat the oil in a saucepan and add the leeks. Cook, stirring, on high heat, until the parts in contact with the saucepan are well browned—they don't need to be cooked through at this stage. Add the slices of duck and cook briefly on both sides. When the meat changes color, add the soup ingredients. Bring to a boil, then lower the heat and let the soup simmer for about 3 minutes.

Meanwhile, cook the soba noodles according to the instructions on the package. Drain the noodles and divide them among four large bowls. Pour the soup over. Arrange the slices of duck and leeks on top. Garnish with the grated radish and yuzu zest.

☀YUZU = 柚子

its zest is used a lot to add fragrance to dishes

CURRY UDON
UDON NOODLES IN CURRY SOUP
カレーうどん

SERVES 4

15 MINS PREPARATION TIME

15–20 MINS COOKING TIME

200 g (7 oz) pork belly,
  thinly sliced
1 tablespoon vegetable oil
1 onion, cut into
  5 mm (¼ in) slices
1.2 liters (42 fl oz)
  dashi (see p. 12)
1 tablespoon mirin
1 tablespoon soy sauce

4 cubes Japanese
  curry sauce mix
  (mild, medium or hot)
320 g (11¼ oz) dried udon
  noodles, or 4 packages
  precooked udon
finely chopped spring
  onion (scallion)

Cut the slices of pork into 3 cm (1¼ in) pieces. Heat the oil in a large saucepan on medium heat and sauté the pork until the meat turns pale. Add the onion and sauté for 1 minute. Add the dashi, mirin and soy sauce and bring to a boil. Reduce the heat to low and cook until the onion is tender. Crumble the curry-sauce-mix cubes and add them to the pan. Cook, stirring regularly, for another 3 minutes until the curry sauce mix blends into the soup and thickens it.

Cook the noodles according to the instructions on the package. Drain the noodles and divide among four bowls. Pour the soup over the noodles. Garnish with the spring onion and serve immediately.

NIKU UDON
UDON WITH SWEET AND SAVORY BEEF
肉うどん

SERVES 4

15 MINS PREPARATION TIME

15–20 MINS COOKING TIME

Amani beef (beef simmered in a sweet sauce)
400 g (14 oz) beef, ideally a well-marbled cut, sliced
2 tablespoons soy sauce
1 tablespoon raw (demerara) sugar
2 tablespoons mirin
200 ml (7 fl oz) dashi (see p. 12)

Soup
1.2 liters (42 fl oz) dashi (see p. 12)
3 tablespoons mirin
3 tablespoons soy sauce
1 teaspoon salt
2 tablespoons sake
320 g (11¼ oz) dried udon noodles,
   or 4 packages precooked udon
1 spring onion (scallion), finely chopped

For the beef, cut the beef slices into 3 cm (1¼ in) strips. Place the beef, soy sauce, sugar and mirin in a saucepan. Sauté, stirring regularly, over low to medium heat. Add the dashi and let it simmer on low heat for 5 minutes.

To make the soup, put all of the ingredients in a saucepan and bring to a boil.

Cook the noodles according to the instructions on the package. Drain the noodles and divide among four bowls. Pour the soup over the noodles. Top with the beef, garnish with the spring onion and serve immediately.

RĀMEN
ラーメン

SERVES 1
10 MINS PREPARATION TIME + **2 HRS** RESTING TIME
15 MINS COOKING TIME
+ TIME TO PREPARE AND COOK THE PORK

4 slices of pork simmered with star anise (see p. 232)
1 egg
2 cm (¾ in) leek (white part),
  thinly sliced on the diagonal
1 tablespoon sesame oil
1 teaspoon soy sauce
freshly ground pepper

Broth
400 ml (14 fl oz) water
4 tablespoons sauce from the pork
1 tablespoon fish sauce
freshly ground pepper
100 g (3½ oz) dried ramen noodles
finely chopped spring onion (scallion)

To prepare the toppings, cut the pork into 1 cm (½ in) thick pieces.
Soft- or hard-boil the egg, according to your preference. If you
have any leftover sauce from the pork, marinate the egg in it
for 2 hours. Combine the leek, sesame oil, soy sauce and some
pepper in a small bowl.

Combine the broth ingredients in a saucepan on medium heat.
Once the broth comes to a boil, lower the heat and keep the
broth hot.

Cook the noodles according to the instructions on the package.
Drain well. Make sure you serve the noodles immediately after
cooking, otherwise they will lose their texture and flavor. Place
the noodles in a large bowl. Pour the hot broth over, then add the
toppings, spring onion and more pepper. It will be scalding hot,
but that's how ramen is enjoyed!

YAKISOBA
JAPANESE FRIED NOODLES
焼きそば

SERVES 4

15 MINS PREPARATION TIME

10 MINS COOKING TIME + COOKING TIME

FOR THE NOODLES IF NECESSARY

4 packages dried ramen
  noodles (about 250 g/9 oz),
  or 4 packages steamed
  "Mushimen" noodles
  (about 520 g/1 lb 2¾ oz)—
  these are ideal for this dish
3 tablespoons sunflower oil
1 onion, cut into
  5 mm (¼ in) slices

200 g (7 oz) pork belly,
  thinly sliced
1 leaf white cabbage,
  cut into bite-size pieces
3 tablespoons tonkatsu sauce
1½ tablespoons oyster sauce
1 teaspoon fish sauce
4 eggs
few pinches aonori*

Cook the dried noodles according to the instructions on the package (skip this step if you are using precooked noodles). Drain.

Heat 1 tablespoon of the oil in a large frying pan on medium heat. Sauté the onion until it becomes translucent, then add the pork and cook for 2 minutes. Add the cabbage and sauté for another minute. Set this mixture aside.

Clean the frying pan, place on medium-high heat and add the remaining 2 tablespoons of oil. Sauté the noodles for 2 minutes, stirring well so they don't stick. Once the noodles are nice and glossy, add the pork and vegetables. Add the sauces and mix together well. Divide among four individual plates. Fry the eggs and place one on top of each plate. Sprinkle with aonori and serve.

* AONORI

green seaweed
powder

often sold in a
triangular
bottle

蕎麦 SOBA MASTERS

03

04

Soba masters make their noodle dough from buckwheat flour.

They use different rolling pins for rolling out, rolling up and unrolling the dough.

They then dust the dough with buckwheat flour before folding it into three layers to cut the noodles.

01

02

05

06

09

07

08

10

SOBA
COOKING

蕎麦を茹でる

01

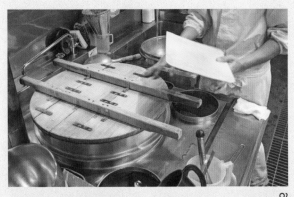

02

03

04

CHA-HAN
JAPANESE FRIED RICE
チャーハン

SERVES 4

5 MINS PREPARATION TIME
10 MINS COOKING TIME

5 eggs
4 tablespoons sunflower oil
4 bowls of cooked rice (see p. 10), cold or lukewarm
1 leek (white part), finely chopped
1 tablespoon soy sauce, plus extra for drizzling
1 tablespoon fish sauce
1 pinch salt
1 tablespoon sake

Break the eggs into a bowl and mix well. Heat a wok on medium heat and add 2 tablespoons of the oil. Pour in the beaten eggs and stir roughly to scramble. When they are softly set, remove from the heat and put aside.

Before frying the rice, use your hands to break up any clumps into more or less separate grains. Place the same wok used for the eggs on high heat. (If your wok is a small one, fry the rice in two batches, otherwise its texture will be very sticky.) Add the remaining 2 tablespoons of oil, and when the pan is quite hot, add the rice. Fry the rice, stirring and turning over constantly with a spatula. Once the grains are coated with oil and well separated, add the leek and the eggs. Continue to stir on high heat, adding the soy sauce, fish sauce, salt and sake, until everything is heated through. To finish, drizzle a little more soy sauce down the sides of the wok, so the rice is well flavored with the caramelized sauce.

OYAKO DON

RICE BOWL WITH CHICKEN AND OMELETTE
親子丼

SERVES 4

15 MINS PREPARATION TIME

7 MINS COOKING TIME (FOR EACH OMELETTE)

250 g (9 oz) chicken breast or thigh fillet
1 leek (white part)
8 eggs, 2 per person
200 ml (7 fl oz) dashi (see p. 12), or water
1 tablespoon sugar

3 tablespoons soy sauce
3 tablespoons mirin*
4 bowls of cooked rice (see p. 10)
nori squares
sliced spring onion (scallion), to garnish

Cut the chicken into 3 cm (1¼ in) cubes. Cut the leek on the diagonal into 1 cm (½ in) slices. Break the eggs into a bowl and mix well. Add the dashi and leek to a frying pan and bring to a boil on medium heat. Add the chicken, sugar, soy sauce and mirin, and continue cooking until the leek is tender and the chicken is cooked. Pour the eggs into the frying pan. Once the eggs start to set, cover and cook for another 30 seconds. Remove from the heat but leave the lid on for a few minutes to let the eggs finish cooking (for an omelette that is still a little runny).

Place the cooked rice in large individual bowls. Divide the omelette into quarters and carefully slide a quarter onto the rice in each bowl. (This is a delicate operation because the semicooked omelette will break up easily.) Garnish with the nori and spring onion. Serve immediately.

Note: You will get better-looking results with this dish if you make individual omelettes. To do this, divide all the ingredients by 4 and cook each batch in a small frying pan.

*MIRIN

= 味醂
a very mild and sweet sake used as a condiment

TENDON
TEMPURA ON RICE
天丼

SERVES 4
30 MINS PREPARATION TIME
30 MINS COOKING TIME

Sauce
2 handfuls katsuobushi*
100 ml (3½ fl oz) soy sauce
100 ml (3½ fl oz) mirin
2 tablespoons raw
   (demerara) sugar
4 cm x 4 cm (1½ in x 1½ in)
   piece kombu seaweed
360 ml (12½ fl oz) water

Tempura batter
1 egg
125 ml (4 fl oz/½ cup)
   very cold water

75 g (2½ oz/½ cup)
   all-purpose flour

8 large raw prawns (shrimp)
¼ white sweet potato
½ green pepper
½ eggplant
vegetable oil, for deep-frying
4 bowls of cooked
   rice (see p. 10)
1 sheet nori seaweed,
   shredded

Place all the sauce ingredients in a saucepan and bring to a boil. Cook on low heat for 15 minutes, then strain. You can keep this sauce in the refrigerator for up to 3 weeks.

For the tempura batter, break the egg into a large bowl. Mix well with the water, then add the flour and lightly mix, leaving it slightly lumpy—this makes for a crispy batter. Set aside in the refrigerator.

Peel and devein the prawns, leaving the tail intact. Cut along the back and a little along the front so the prawns stay flat when they're cooked. Cut the sweet potato into 6 mm (¼ in) slices, and the pepper and eggplant into 4 pieces. Heat the oil in a saucepan to 170°C (325°F). Dip the vegetables in the batter and deep-fry until golden and cooked through, then drain on paper towels. Raise the temperature of the oil to 180°C (350°F). Holding the prawns by their tails, dip them in the batter one at a time and deep-fry until golden and just cooked, then drain on paper towels.

Serve the rice in four large individual bowls, each dressed with a tablespoon of the sauce. Place some shredded nori and the tempura on the rice, then drizzle over another 2 tablespoons of the sauce.

✳ KATSUOBUSHI
= dried bonito
   flakes

MAGURO AVOCADO DON

MARINATED TUNA WITH AVOCADO AND RICE

マグロアボカド丼

SERVES 4

25 MINS PREPARATION TIME

Marinade
1 small garlic clove
4 tablespoons soy sauce
2 tablespoons mirin
2 teaspoons sesame oil

250 g (9 oz) sashimi-grade tuna fillet,
  cut into 2 cm (¾ in) cubes
1 ripe avocado
4 bowls of cooked rice (see p. 10)
1 sheet nori seaweed, torn into 1 cm (½ in) squares

To make the marinade, grate the garlic and combine with the soy sauce, mirin and sesame oil.

Add the tuna to the marinade and marinate for 15 minutes.

Just before serving, cut the avocado into 2 cm (¾ in) cubes. Place the rice in individual bowls and top with the tuna and avocado. Spoon a tablespoon of the marinade over the rice and garnish with the nori.

Note: Cut up the avocado at the last minute so it doesn't oxidize.

SPAGHETTI NAPOLITAN
ナポリタン

SERVES 4

15 MINS PREPARATION TIME
15 MINS COOKING TIME

360 g (12¾ oz) spaghetti
30 g (1 oz) butter
1 onion, cut into 5 mm (¼ in) slices
½ green pepper, cut into 5 mm (¼ in) pieces
½ red pepper, cut into 5 mm (¼ in) pieces
6 mushrooms, cut into 5 mm (¼ in) slices
100 g (3½ oz) pork sausage, such as frankfurter
 cut into rounds
165 g (5¾ oz) tomato sauce
sea salt
freshly ground pepper
finely grated parmesan cheese

Cook the spaghetti for the length of time indicated on the package.

Melt the butter in a saucepan. Add the onion, peppers, mushrooms and sausage and cook until golden brown. Add the spaghetti and tomato sauce, season with salt and pepper and mix together well. When everything is heated through, divide the spaghetti napolitan among the four plates, sprinkle with parmesan cheese and serve immediately.

TARAKO
SPAGHETTI

タラコスパゲッティー

SERVES 4
5 MINS PREPARATION TIME
10 MINS COOKING TIME

400 g (14 oz) spaghetti
100 g (3½ oz) tarako*
50 g (1¾ oz) salted butter
1 shiso (perilla) or basil leaf, finely shredded
sea salt

Cook the spaghetti in salted water as indicated on the package.

Meanwhile, empty the packages of tarako into a mixing bowl and add the butter. Drain the pasta and add to the bowl. Mix together well, then divide among four individual plates. Garnish with the shiso or basil and serve immediately.

✳ TARAKO

= 鱈子 salted cod
or Alaska pollock roe

When it is prepared
with chili, it is called
"MENTAI-KO"

NIGIRI ZUSHI
MIXED SUSHI
にぎり寿司

SERVES 4

30 MINS PREPARATION TIME

+ TIME TO PREPARE THE SUSHI RICE

Toppings
4 large raw prawns (shrimp)
1 piece sashimi-grade tuna
  fillet, about 5 cm x 4 cm
  (2 in x 1½ in)
1 fillet sashimi-grade
  gilthead bream
4 fillets sashimi-grade
  Japanese horse mackerel
4 tablespoons salmon roe

vinegared sushi rice
  (see p. 237), made with
  300 g (10½ oz) rice
wasabi
1 sheet of nori seaweed
soy sauce

Prepare the toppings. Remove the heads of the prawns. Insert skewers along their backs and cook them in boiling water for 4 minutes, then remove the skewers. Peel the prawns and carefully split open their belly without cutting them in half. Cut the tuna into slices 1 cm (½ in) thick, 2.5 cm (1 in) wide and about 5 cm (2 in) long. Slice the bream in the same way. Remove the skin of the horse mackerel.

Use your hand to shape the rice into small oval balls (20 in total). Place a prawn or a slice of fish in the hollow of your hand. Dab a little wasabi in the middle of the slice, then place the ball of rice on top. Turn the ball of rice and fish over, so the fish is now on top. Press lightly in the middle with your index and middle fingers. With the sushi still sitting in the hollow of your hand, use your thumb and middle finger to squeeze the edges firmly, then press your index finger on top of the sushi to flatten it slightly. To make sushi with the salmon roe, cut the sheet of nori into strips about 20 cm x 3 cm (8 in x 1¼ in). Wrap a strip of nori around a ball of rice, securing the ends with a cooked grain of rice so it sticks properly. Place the salmon roe on top of the rice ball—the rim of the nori should hold it in place. Serve with soy sauce.

66

INARI ZUSHI
FRIED TOFU STUFFED WITH SUSHI RICE
いなり寿司

SERVES 4

30 MINS PREPARATION TIME + TIME TO PREPARE THE SUSHI RICE

20 MINS COOKING TIME

8 abura-age*
200 ml (7 fl oz) dashi (see p. 12)
3 tablespoons soy sauce
3 tablespoons raw (demerara) sugar
1 tablespoon mirin
a bowl filled with equal amounts of water and vinegar
vinegared sushi rice (see p. 237),
  made with 300 g (10½ oz) rice

Cut each abura-age in half crosswise to give you 2 squares, then open up the pockets. Bring a large saucepan of water to a boil. Add the abura-age and cook for 2 minutes to remove the excess oil. Drain, and when they're cool enough to handle, squeeze between your hands to remove the water and oil. Place the dashi, soy sauce, sugar and mirin in a saucepan. Mix together well and bring to a boil. Add the abura-age and simmer, covered, for 10 to 15 minutes, on medium heat. Once the abura-age has absorbed the sauce, turn off the heat. Allow to cool.

Moisten your hands with the vinegared water. Reopen the abura-age pockets. Take a small amount of sushi rice and fill the pocket, leaving some space at the top. Fold the edges over each other to close. Arrange the inari zushi, seam side down, on a plate. You can eat these plain, without soy sauce.

*ABURA—AGE
= 油揚げ

fried rectangular-shaped sheets of tofu

KATSU SANDO
BREADED PORK SANDWICH
カツサンド

SERVES 4

15 MINS PREPARATION TIME
+ TIME TO PREPARE THE TONKATSU

Coleslaw
⅛ white cabbage
a few herb leaves, such as shiso (perilla),
    mint and coriander (cilantro)
1 tablespoon olive oil
juice of ½ organic lemon
1 pinch salt

8 slices sandwich bread
2–3 tablespoons whole-grain mustard
4 tablespoons mayonnaise
¼ cucumber, sliced
4 tonkatsu (see p. 210)
4 tablespoons tonkatsu sauce

To make the coleslaw, use a mandoline to thinly slice the cabbage.
Finely chop the herbs. Combine the cabbage, herbs, olive oil,
lemon juice and salt in a bowl and leave to marinate for 5 minutes.

Toast the bread. Spread two slices of bread with mustard and
mayonnaise. Place the following, in order, on one of the slices:
cucumber slices, tonkatsu, 1 tablespoon tonkatsu sauce and a
quarter of the coleslaw. Top with the other slice of bread. Repeat
the process for each sandwich.

TERIYAKI CHICKEN BURGER
照り焼きバーガー

SERVES 4
20 MINS PREPARATION TIME
10 MINS COOKING TIME

Teriyaki chicken
2 tablespoons soy sauce
2 tablespoons mirin
1 teaspoon honey
flour, for dusting
4 boneless chicken thighs
vegetable oil, for frying

Coleslaw
¼ red cabbage
⅛ red onion
½ carrot, peeled
1 tablespoon rice vinegar
1 tablespoon olive oil

1 tablespoon raw
   (demerara) sugar
1 tablespoon salt
1 tablespoon mayonnaise

4 burger buns, cut in half
a few leaves of
   iceberg lettuce
4 rounded teaspoons
   mayonnaise
½ red onion, thinly sliced
   and separated into rings
4 teaspoons ketchup

For the teriyaki chicken, combine the soy sauce, mirin and honey in a small bowl. Lightly flour the chicken. Heat 1 tablespoon of oil in a frying pan on medium heat and cook the chicken for 3 minutes on each side. Pour in the sauce, then bring to a boil to thicken and stir to coat the chicken.

To make the coleslaw, slice the cabbage and red onion very thinly. Cut the carrot into matchsticks. Combine with the rest of the coleslaw ingredients and marinate for 5 minutes.

Warm the buns in the oven. Fill each bun with, in order, lettuce, mayonnaise, chicken, coleslaw, onion and ketchup.

食品サンプル

SHOKUHIN SANPURU

The Japanese love images and like to see what they are going to eat before taking a table.

Restaurants offering standard menus pay high prices for ready-made fake dishes. Because everything is painstakingly made by hand, these fakes don't come cheap.

Today, restaurants tend to change their menus frequently and create innovative dishes, so they need custom-made fake dishes that are faithful to the original. As these are ever more expensive, fake food is often replaced by photographs these days.

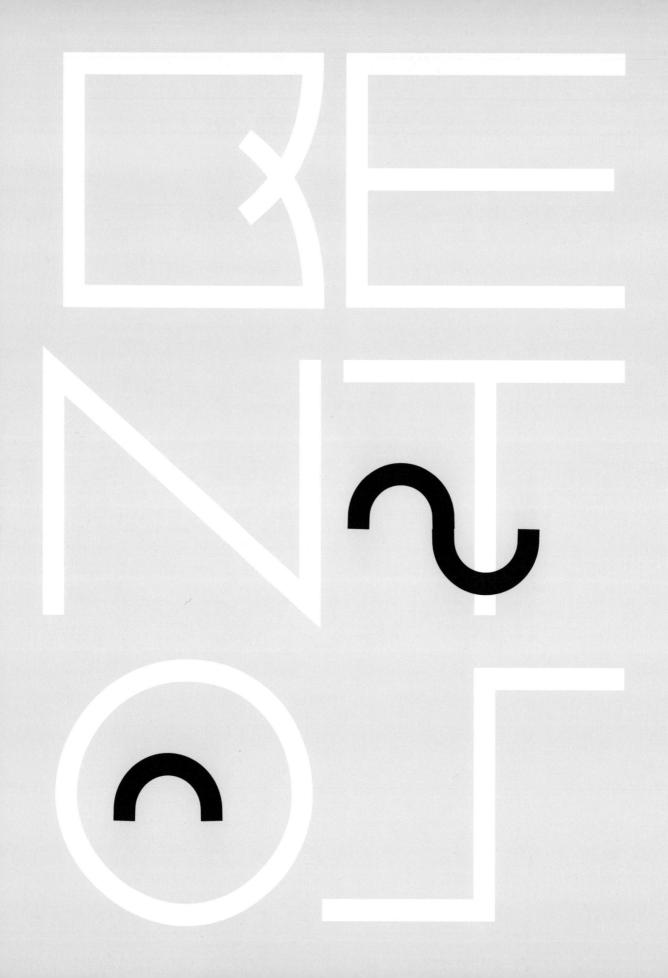

弁 当

BENTO

A bento box contains protein, fresh or pickled vegetables and rice, sometimes in the form of rice balls (**onigiri**). It is a meal for workers, students and travelers. Each major train station has its own **eki bento**, or ekiben. The bento also follows the rhythms of nature with the **kouraku bento**, the "picnic bento." A **hanami bento** is eaten while contemplating the beauty of blossoming cherry trees. The traditional Japanese kabuki theater also has its own bento, the **makuno uchi bento**, enjoyed during intermissions.

HANAMI BENTO
花見弁当

SERVES 4
1 HR PREPARATION TIME
1 HR COOKING TIME
3 HRS RESTING TIME
+ TIME TO PREPARE AND COOK THE RICE

CHIRASHI ZUSHI

HOURENSO (spinach)

KARA-AGE (chicken)

EBI (prawns)

TSUKUNE (chicken meatballs)

CHIRASHI ZUSHI
RICE WITH TOPPINGS
ちらし寿司

30 MINS PREPARATION TIME
3 HRS RESTING TIME
20 MINS COOKING TIME
+ TIME TO PREPARE AND COOK THE SUSHI RICE

5–6 dried shiitake
  mushrooms
1 package of lotus root
  (about 200 g/7 oz)
2 tablespoons rice vinegar
1 carrot
1 tablespoon first cold-
  pressed sesame oil
100 ml (3½ fl oz) dashi
  (see p. 12)
2 tablespoons mirin
3 tablespoons soy sauce
2 tablespoons sugar

4 eggs
sunflower oil, for frying
½ bunch nano-hana*
  or arugula
1 teaspoon salt
1 jar salmon roe
  (about 100 g/3½ oz)
2 tablespoons toasted
  sesame seeds
vinegared sushi rice
  (see p. 237), prepared
  with 450 g (1 lb) rice

Place the dried shiitake mushrooms in a bowl, cover with water and leave to soak for at least 3 hours. When they are soft, drain them, reserving the liquid. (You could also soak them overnight, placing the bowl in the refrigerator.) Remove the stems and cut the caps into 5 mm (¼ in) slices. Peel and slice the lotus root into 2 mm (¹⁄₁₆in) rounds, then soak for 10 minutes in water with 1 tablespoon of rice vinegar added to it. Drain. Cut the carrot into 3 cm (1¼ in) lengths, then into thin matchsticks.

Heat the sesame oil in a saucepan on medium heat. Add the lotus root, sliced shiitakes and carrot and sauté for 1 minute. Add the dashi, mirin, 2 tablespoons of soy sauce, 1 tablespoon of sugar, the remaining 1 tablespoon of rice vinegar and 100 ml (3½ fl oz) of the shiitake soaking liquid. Cook for about 15 minutes on low heat, stirring from time to time. Once the liquid has reduced and thickened, remove from the heat and allow to cool.

Break the eggs into a bowl and add the remaining1 tablespoon of sugar and 1 tablespoon of soy sauce. Heat a frying pan on medium heat and coat with sunflower oil, wiping away the excess with a paper towel. Make thin omelettes in several batches. Stack the omelettes on top of each other and cut into three, then into thin strips. Have ready a large bowl of iced water. Cook the nano-hana for 1 minute in a saucepan of salted boiling water. Drain and drop in the iced water to cool it down quickly. Drain again and lightly squeeze out the liquid between your hands. Cut into 3 cm (1¼ in) lengths.

Combine two-thirds of the lotus root, shiitake and carrot mixture and their cooking liquid with the sesame seeds and the sushi rice. Place the sushi rice in a large bento box. Arrange the rest of the cooked vegetables on top and garnish with the omelette, salmon roe and nano-hana.

✳NANO-HANA

= 菜の花 very similar
   to mustard leaves
you can find it in
Chinese supermarkets

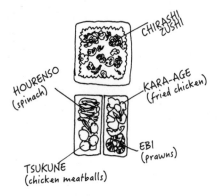

CHIRASHI ZUSHI

HOURENSO (spinach)

KARA-AGE (fried chicken)

EBI (prawns)

TSUKUNE (chicken meatballs)

HOURENSO NO GOMA AE
SPINACH WITH SESAME SAUCE
ほうれん草の胡麻和え

5 MINS PREPARATION TIME
2 MINS COOKING TIME

150 g (5½ oz) spinach, leaves and stems
1 teaspoon salt
1 tablespoon soy sauce
1 teaspoon raw (demerara) sugar
1 tablespoon white sesame paste (tahini)
1 teaspoon toasted sesame seeds

Cook the spinach in boiling salted water for barely 1 minute. Drain, and when it is cool enough to handle, use your hands to squeeze out the water. Cut the spinach into 3 cm (1¼ in) lengths. Combine the soy sauce, sugar, sesame paste and sesame seeds in a small bowl, then add the spinach.

TSUKUNE
CHICKEN MEATBALLS
つくね

Make the recipe on p. 184, halving the quantities. Shape into smaller balls (about 3 cm/1¼ in across).

EBI NO KOUSAI AE
PRAWNS WITH CILANTRO
海老の香菜和え

SERVES 4
15 MINS PREPARATION TIME
4 MINS COOKING TIME

Sauce
½ bunch cilantro
1 small thumb-size piece of ginger
½ garlic clove
2 tablespoons fish sauce
1 pinch raw (demerara) sugar
100 ml (3½ fl oz) first cold-pressed sesame oil
  or sunflower oil
juice of ¼ lime

12 large raw prawns (shrimp)
coarse salt

Blend all the sauce ingredients in a food processor. Remove the heads of the prawns. Peel and devein the prawns, leaving the tails intact. Cook in boiling water with a pinch of coarse salt. Drain well and combine with 3 tablespoons of sauce.

KARA-AGE
FRIED CHICKEN
唐揚げ

Make the recipe on p. 150, halving the quantities. Cut the pieces of chicken into smaller cubes (about 3 cm/1¼ in).

FISH
BENTO
魚弁当

SERVES 2

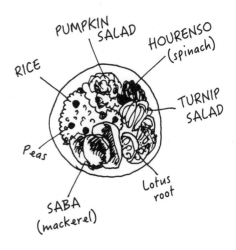

RICE
PUMPKIN SALAD
HOURENSO (spinach)
TURNIP SALAD
Peas
Lotus root
SABA (mackerel)

SABA NO TATSUTA AGE
DEEP-FRIED MARINATED MACKEREL
鯖の竜田揚げ

5 MINS PREPARATION TIME
10 MINS COOKING TIME

2 x 200 g (7 oz) mackerel fillets
2 teaspoons soy sauce
1 teaspoon grated ginger
4 tablespoons potato starch
sunflower oil, for deep-frying

Cut the mackerel fillets into 3 pieces. Marinate them in the soy sauce and ginger in a small bowl for 10 minutes. Dry with paper towels. Dust with potato starch, then deep-fry in a small saucepan and drain.

TURNIP AND YELLOW BEETROOT SALAD
蕪と黄蕪のサラダ

5 MINS PREPARATION TIME
20–30 MINS COOKING TIME

1 yellow beetroot (beet)
1 turnip
1 teaspoon unrefined salt
1 teaspoon sesame oil
1 teaspoon rice vinegar

Cook the beetroot, then peel and slice thinly using a mandoline. Slice the turnip in the same way. Combine with the rest of the ingredients.

RICE WITH PEAS
豆ご飯

5 MINS PREPARATION TIME
5 MINS COOKING TIME

50 g (1¾ oz) peas
1 teaspoon salt
2 bowls of cooked rice (see p. 10)

Cook the peas in a saucepan of salted water. Drain and combine with the rice.

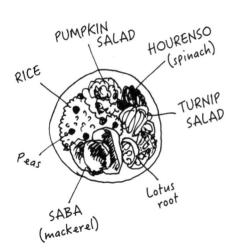

RICE
PUMPKIN SALAD
HOURENSO (spinach)
TURNIP SALAD
Peas
Lotus root
SABA (mackerel)

HOURENSO NO KARASHI AE

SPINACH WITH JAPANESE MUSTARD

ほうれん草の
芥子和え

5 MINS PREPARATION TIME
2 MINS COOKING TIME

150 g (5½ oz) spinach,
  leaves and stems
1 teaspoon salt
1 tablespoon soy sauce
1 teaspoon Japanese mustard

Cook the spinach in boiling salted water
for barely 1 minute. Drain, and when
it is cool enough to handle, use your
hands to squeeze out the water. Cut
the spinach into 3 cm (1¼ in) lengths.
Combine the soy sauce and mustard in
a small bowl, add the spinach and mix.

PUMPKIN SALAD

南瓜サラダ

5 MINS PREPARATION TIME
10 MINS COOKING TIME

200 g (7 oz) pumpkin
1 tablespoon black raisins
4 mint leaves, chopped
1 rounded teaspoon chopped onion
1 teaspoon olive oil
squeeze of organic lemon juice
1 pinch salt
1 small pinch curry powder
1 small pinch sugar
1 tablespoon mayonnaise

Peel and cut the pumpkin into 2 cm (¾
in) chunks. Place in a saucepan with
100 ml (3½ fl oz) of water and place
over low to medium heat. Cover and
cook the pumpkin in the steam from
the water. If the water evaporates
before the pumpkin is cooked, add a
little more. While the pumpkin is still
hot, combine it with the rest of the
ingredients except for the mayonnaise.
Once the pumpkin salad has cooled, stir
in the mayonnaise.

DEEP-FRIED LOTUS ROOT WITH SESAME SEEDS

揚げ蓮根の
胡麻和え

10 MINS PREPARATION TIME
10 MINS COOKING TIME

6 cm (2½ in) lotus root
sunflower oil, for deep-frying
1 tablespoon soy sauce
1 tablespoon sesame seeds

Peel and halve the lotus root, then
slice into 6 mm (¼ in) pieces. Soak in
water for 5 minutes, then drain. Dry the
lotus root on paper towels. In a small
saucepan, heat a 2 cm (¾ in) depth of
oil to about 170°C (425°F). Deep-fry the
pieces of lotus root until they are nice
and golden. Drain and combine with the
soy sauce and sesame seeds.

MEAT BENTO
肉弁当

SERVES 1

KATSUDON

CUCUMBER

RICE
UNDERNEATH

* SHICHIMI
= 七味
Japanese spice mix
with 7 ingredients

(mandarin zest,
sesame seeds, sansho
pepper, red chili...)

KATSUDON
BREADED PORK
OMELETTE ON RICE
カツ丼

10 MINS PREPARATION TIME
10 MINS COOKING TIME
+ **20 MINS** TO PREPARE AND COOK THE TONKATSU

1 piece tonkatsu
  (see p. 210)
2 eggs
¼ onion
50 ml (1¾ fl oz) dashi
  (see p. 12) or water

1 teaspoon sugar
2 teaspoons mirin
1 tablespoon soy sauce
1 bowl of cooked
  rice (see p. 10)
shichimi*

Slice the tonkatsu into 2 cm (¾ in) strips. Break the eggs into a bowl and mix. Peel and cut the onion into 5 mm (¼ in) slices. Add the dashi and onion to a small frying pan and bring to a boil on medium heat. Add the sugar, mirin and soy sauce, and continue cooking until the onion is tender. Add the pieces of tonkatsu and cook for another 2 minutes, then add the eggs. Once the eggs start to set, cover the pan and cook for another 30 seconds. Remove from the heat but leave the lid on for a few minutes to let the eggs finish cooking (for an omelette that is still a little runny).

Serve the rice in a bento box. Carefully slide the omelette onto the rice, then sprinkle with shichimi.

PICKLED CUCUMBER
キュウリの和え物

5 MINS PREPARATION TIME

3 cm (1¼ in) cucumber, thinly sliced
  on the diagonal
1 teaspoon salt
1 cm (½ in) piece kombu seaweed
1 thin slice ginger, cut into matchsticks

Combine all the ingredients in a small bowl and marinate until ready to serve. Drain and serve alongside the katsudon.

VEGETABLE BENTO
野菜弁当

SERVES 1

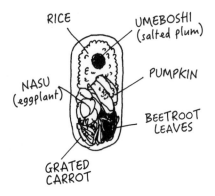

RICE

UMEBOSHI
(salted plum)

NASU
(eggplant)

PUMPKIN

BEETROOT
LEAVES

GRATED
CARROT

NASU NO MISO ITAME
SAUTÉED EGGPLANT WITH MISO
茄子の味噌炒め

3 MINS PREPARATION TIME
5 MINS COOKING TIME

1 tablespoon miso
1 tablespoon mirin
1 teaspoon raw (demerara) sugar
1 tablespoon sesame oil
½ eggplant, cut into 2 cm (¾ in) cubes
3 tablespoons water
¼ green pepper, seeded
  and cut into 2 cm (¾ in) cubes

Combine the miso, mirin and sugar in a small bowl. Heat the oil in a small saucepan on low heat, then add the eggplant and sauté for 1 minute. Add the water, cover the saucepan and cook until the eggplant is tender. Add the pepper and the miso mixture. Combine well, then remove from the heat.

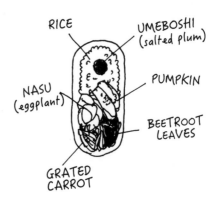

RICE
UMEBOSHI
(salted plum)
NASU
(eggplant)
PUMPKIN
BEETROOT
LEAVES
GRATED
CARROT

SAUTÉED BEETROOT LEAVES
赤蕪の葉の炒め物

3 MINS PREPARATION TIME
3 MINS COOKING TIME

1 teaspoon olive oil
1 handful beetroot leaves and stems,
   well washed and cut into 3 cm (1¼ in) strips
   (you can use spinach as a substitute)
1 teaspoon oyster sauce
freshly ground pepper

Heat the oil in a frying pan on medium heat and sauté the beetroot leaves and stems until tender. Add the oyster sauce and pepper. Remove from the heat.

BAKED PUMPKIN
南瓜のオーブン焼き

3 MINS PREPARATION TIME
8 MINS COOKING TIME

1 teaspoon sunflower oil
1 teaspoon soy sauce
1 teaspoon honey
1 pinch salt
4 x 5 mm (¼ in) slices peeled pumpkin
1 rounded tablespoon panko breadcrumbs

Preheat the oven to 180°C (350°F). Mix the oil, soy sauce, honey and salt in a bowl. Add the pumpkin and mix to coat. Lay the slices of pumpkin on a baking sheet and sprinkle the panko on top. Bake for 8 to10 minutes until tender.

GRATED CARROT
キャロットラペ

5 MINS PREPARATION TIME

½ carrot, peeled and grated
1 teaspoon sesame oil
1 teaspoon rice vinegar
½ teaspoon soy sauce
1 pinch sunflower seeds
1 teaspoon raisins

Combine all the ingredients in a bowl and leave to marinate for 5 minutes.

RICE WITH UMEBOSHI
日の丸ご飯

TIME TO PREPARE AND COOK THE RICE

1 umeboshi (salted plum)
1 bowl of cooked rice (see p. 10)

Place the umeboshi in the middle of the cooked rice. You can find umeboshi in Japanese grocery stores. This plum is often used in bentos because it has antibacterial properties and is considered to be very good for overall health because it alkalizes the blood.

お握り

ONIGIRI
RICE
BALLS

METHOD

SERVES 4–6

1 LARGE ONIGIRI = **2 SMALL** ONIGIRI = **1 BOWL** COOKED RICE

1. Thoroughly wet your hands.
2. Place 1 pinch of salt in your palm.
3. Take some rice in the other hand.
4. Place your chosen ingredient (optional) in the center.
5. Shape into a ball with the other hand, pushing the ingredient inside the ball. Add a little more rice on top to cover, if needed.
6. Form into a triangle, neatly shaping each corner.

01

03

04

05

07

06

08

09

VARIOUS ONIGIRI
RICE BALLS
お握り

SERVES 4–6

GROUND PORK AND GINGER ONIGIRI
挽肉と生姜のお握り

MAKES 8 SMALL ONIGIRI
5 MINS PREPARATION TIME
10 MINS COOKING TIME

vegetable oil, for frying
200 g (7 oz) ground pork belly
2 cm (¾ in) piece ginger,
  finely chopped
1 tablespoon soy sauce
2 teaspoons raw (demerara) sugar
1 tablespoon mirin
2 tablespoons sake
freshly ground pepper
4 bowls of cooked rice (see p. 10)

Heat the oil in a small frying pan on medium heat. Sauté the pork and ginger. Once the pork changes color, add the rest of the ingredients except for the rice. Cook, stirring with a spatula, until the liquid has almost evaporated. Combine with the rice. Make the onigiri according to the instructions on p. 94.

EGG AND YUKARI ONIGIRI
ゆかりお握り

MAKES 8 SMALL ONIGIRI
5 MINS PREPARATION TIME
5 MINS COOKING TIME

2 eggs
1 teaspoon raw (demerara) sugar
2 tablespoons yukari
  (Japanese condiment made
  from red shiso)
4 bowls of cooked rice (see p. 10)

Break the eggs into a bowl and add the sugar. Mix together well. Heat a small frying pan and scramble the eggs. Combine the yukari and eggs with the rice. Make the onigiri according to the instructions on p. 94.

OKAKA ONIGIRI
おかかお握り

MAKES 8 SMALL ONIGIRI
3 MINS PREPARATION TIME

5 g (⅛ oz) katsuobushi
  (dried bonito flakes)
½ tablespoon soy sauce
4 bowls of cooked rice (see p. 10)

Combine the katsuobushi with the soy sauce, then mix with the rice. Make the onigiri according to the instructions on p. 94.

VARIOUS ONIGIRI (CONTINUED)

ONIGIRI WITH PEAS
豆ご飯お握り

MAKES 8 SMALL ONIGIRI
5 MINS PREPARATION TIME
10 MINS COOKING TIME

150 g (5½ oz) peas in their pods
1 teaspoon salt
4 bowls of cooked rice (see p. 10)
1 cm (½ in) piece ginger,
  peeled and finely chopped

Shuck the peas and cook them in salted water. Drain and combine with the rice and ginger. Make the onigiri according to the instructions on p. 94.

ONIGIRI WITH SALTED SALMON AND GREENS
青菜と鮭のお握り

MAKES 8 SMALL ONIGIRI
15 MINS PREPARATION TIME
+ 2 HRS RESTING TIME
10 MINS COOKING TIME

1 handful greens, such as beetroot
  (beet) leaves, spinach, turnip leaves
1 teaspoon sesame oil
1 pinch salt
1 salted salmon fillet
  (see p. 24), flaked
1 tablespoon toasted sesame seeds
4 bowls of cooked rice (see p. 10)

Roughly chop the greens. In a small saucepan, heat the oil and sauté the greens. Season with the salt, then remove from the heat. Combine the salmon with the greens, sesame seeds and rice. Make the onigiri according to the instructions on p. 94.

YAKI ONIGIRI
焼きお握り

MAKES 4 LARGE ONIGIRI
5 MINS PREPARATION TIME
15 MINS COOKING TIME

vegetable oil, such as sesame,
  canola or olive, for frying
4 large plain onigiri
  (see p. 94)
2 tablespoons soy sauce

Heat a lightly oiled frying pan on a medium heat (or, even better, use the barbecue). Cook the onigiri on both sides until nice and brown. Brush one side with soy sauce and cook a little longer until the sauce is well browned. Do the same on the other side.

Note: Make sure you make very firm onigiri for this dish so they keep their shape during the cooking.

煎餅 SENBEI CRACKERS

Senbei are savory crackers that are very common in Japan, eaten after meals with tea or as a snack.

This senbei store is one of the best in the Nezu district, a part of Tokyo known for its traditional shops. The senbei makers grill the dried rice crackers and brush them with soy sauce from time to time. The crunch of the well-browned senbei and the flavor of the caramelized sauce are simply delicious.

おやつ

OYATSU

SNACKS

We prefer to eat sweet things for snacks. Traditional sweets compete with Western-inspired cakes called yougashi. **Dorayaki**: filled pancakes. **Mitsumame**: fruit, agar-agar and beans in syrup. **Daifuku-mochi**: stuffed rice cakes. **Shortcake**: Japanese strawberry shortcake. **Roll cake:** a Swiss roll–type cake. **Chiffon cake:** a very light cake. Paradoxically, Japanese sweets are very dense and sweet, but Western-style cakes are expected to be extremely light.

MITARASHI DANGO

RICE BALLS IN SYRUP
みたらし団子

MAKES 5 SKEWERS (20 RICE BALLS)
15 MINS PREPARATION TIME
10 MINS COOKING TIME

150 g (5½ oz) silken tofu
100 g (3½ oz) shiratama-ko (Japanese glutinous
  rice flour, available in Asian grocery stores)

Mitarashi syrup
125 ml (4 fl oz/½ cup) water
40 g (1½ oz) raw (demerara) sugar
3 tablespoons soy sauce
1 tablespoon mirin
1 tablespoon potato starch

Knead the tofu and rice flour together, mashing the tofu well with your hands. Once the mixture forms a smooth dough, shape it into a log. Divide into 20 pieces and roll the pieces into small balls.* Cook the balls in boiling water: once they rise to the surface, cook for a further 2 minutes. Transfer the cooked rice balls to a bowl of cold water to cool them down quickly. Drain, then thread 4 balls onto a skewer. Char the surface of the balls on a wire grilling rack, either on the barbecue or over a gas ring. If you don't have a grilling rack, you can char them on high heat in a dry frying pan.

To make the syrup, place all the ingredients in a saucepan and bring to a boil, stirring constantly with a wooden spatula. Reduce the heat to low and continue to stir and cook for another minute until the syrup becomes thick and clear. Roll the skewers in the syrup so the balls are well coated.

✳ To make the balls

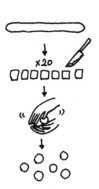

DAIFUKU MOCHI
STUFFED RICE CAKES
大福餅

MAKES 8

30 MINS PREPARATION TIME

1 HR 15 MINS COOKING TIME

200 g (7 oz) koshian*
100 g (3½ oz) shiratama-ko
   (glutinous rice flour)
60 g (2 oz) sugar
1 teaspoon fine salt

150 ml (5 fl oz) water
3 tablespoons cooked
   adzuki beans (see p. 110)
potato starch, for dusting

Divide the koshian paste into 8 portions, then shape into balls using two spoons. Set aside on a plate in the refrigerator. Combine the rice flour, sugar, salt and water in a microwave-safe bowl. Heat in the microwave oven for 2 minutes at 600 watts. Take out and mix with a wet spatula, then heat for another 40 seconds to 1 minute. The dough should now be translucent. Incorporate the adzuki beans.

Dust a baking sheet with enough potato starch to completely cover the surface, then place the dough on the sheet. Dust the surface of the dough with potato starch. Divide into 8 pieces with a dough cutter. The dough needs to be worked while it is still hot, but be careful not to burn yourself. Take the balls of koshian out of the refrigerator. Stretch a piece of the dough with your hands until it is big enough to wrap around a ball of koshian. Place the piece of dough in the hollow of your hand, dust off any excess potato starch and put a ball of koshian in the middle. Close the dough over the koshian, pinching the edges together to seal. Place the stuffed rice cake, seam side down, on a plate dusted with potato starch. Make the others in the same way.

Note: Traditionally, kuromame (black soya beans) are used for these, but they can be difficult to find outside of Japan, so I've replaced them with adzuki beans.

✳ KOSHIAN

＝漉し餡
Adzuki bean paste.
The beans are crushed
and passed through
a fine sieve.

MATCHA
AND WHITE
CHOCOLATE CAKE
抹茶のケーキ

MAKES 1 LOAF CAKE
15 MINS PREPARATION TIME
40 MINS COOKING TIME

3 eggs
softened butter—the same weight as the eggs
caster (superfine) sugar—the same weight as the eggs
all-purpose flour—the same weight as the eggs
1 teaspoon baking powder
1 tablespoon matcha (green tea powder)
70 g (2½ oz) white chocolate chips

Preheat the oven to 170°C (325°F), and butter and flour a 19 x
19 x 8 cm (7½ x 7½ x 3¼ in) loaf pan. Weigh the eggs, then weigh
out the same amount of butter, sugar and flour. Using an electric
mixer, beat the sugar and butter together for 5 minutes, or until
light and creamy. Add the eggs, one at a time, mixing each one in
well before adding the next. Sift in the flour, baking powder and
matcha. Combine using a spatula. Stir in the white chocolate
chips, then pour the mixture into the prepared pan and bake for
40 minutes. The cake is cooked when a toothpick inserted in the
center comes out clean.

MITSUMAME
FRUIT, AGAR-AGAR AND BEANS IN SYRUP
みつ豆

SERVES 4

30 MINS PREPARATION TIME
1 HR 20 MINS COOKING TIME

✳ TSUBUAN

= 粒餡

Adzuki bean paste.
The beans are left whole.

Jelly
2 teaspoons agar-agar
500 ml (17 fl oz/
  2 cups) water
1 tablespoon caster
  (superfine) sugar

110 g (3¾ oz/½ cup)
  dried adzuki bean
2 pinches coarse salt
200 g (7 oz) tsubuan*

1 mandarin orange, peeled
¼ apple, cut into 4 slices
4 x 1.5 cm (⅝ in) rice balls
  (see p. 104), ungrilled
  and without syrup

4 tablespoons
  black sugar sauce
  (see p. 134)
4 cherries in syrup

For the jelly, place the agar-agar and water in a saucepan on medium heat. Bring to a boil, stirring with a wooden spatula. When it boils, keep cooking and stirring for 2 minutes, then add the sugar and stir to dissolve. Remove from the heat and pour into a 15 cm (6 in) square mold or baking pan. Allow to cool at room temperature, then place in the refrigerator. Once the jelly has set, unmold it and cut into 1 cm (½ in) cubes.

Place the adzuki beans in a saucepan and cover with water. Bring to a boil on high heat, then discard the water. Repeat this process. Bring the beans to a boil for a third time, then add the salt and reduce the heat to low. Cook the beans for about 50 minutes, topping up with water as needed to keep them covered. The beans are done when they can be easily crushed between two fingers. Remove from the heat and drain.

In each of four small bowls, place a quarter of the jelly cubes, a quarter of the tsubuan, 1 tablespoon of adzuki beans, a few segments of orange, a slice of apple and a rice ball. Spoon over 1 tablespoon of black sugar sauce and decorate with the cherries.

Note: Traditionally, dried red peas are used for this recipe, but these are hard to find, so I've replaced them with dried adzuki beans.

DORAYAKI
FILLED JAPANESE PANCAKES
どら焼き

MAKES 8
10 MINS PREPARATION TIME + **30 MINS** RESTING TIME
5 MINS COOKING TIME PER BATCH

3 eggs
140 g (5 oz) sugar
1 tablespoon honey
1 tablespoon mirin
1 tablespoon baking soda
  + 3 tablespoons water
185 g (6½ oz/1¼ cups) cake flour
  or all-purpose flour
3 tablespoons water
sunflower oil
400 g (14 oz) tsubuan*

Break the eggs into a mixing bowl and add the sugar, honey and mirin. Whisk together using a hand whisk. Blend the baking soda with the 3 tablespoons of water, then add to the batter, along with the flour. Mix together with a spatula, then leave the batter to rest for 30 minutes. Stir in 3 tablespoons of water to loosen.

Heat a frying pan on medium heat. Lower the heat and lightly oil the pan, wiping away any excess with a paper towel. Pour a small ladleful of batter into the frying pan, to make a pancake about 9 cm (3½ in) across. Cook until bubbles appear on the surface, which should be dry. Turn the pancake over and cook for 1 minute. Make 16 pancakes this way (if you have a large frying pan, you can cook several at once). Set the cooked pancakes aside and cover with plastic wrap so they don't dry out. Sandwich pairs of pancakes with the tsubuan.

* TSUBUAN
= 粒餡
Adzuki bean paste. The beans are left whole.

PURIN
CRÈME CARAMEL
プリン

MAKES 4
15 MINS PREPARATION TIME
13 MINS COOKING TIME

Caramel sauce
70 g (2½ oz) white sugar
3 tablespoons cold water
  + 1 tablespoon hot water

4 eggs
¼ vanilla bean
375 ml (13 fl oz/1½ cups) milk
50 g (1¾ oz) raw
  (demerara) sugar

Lightly oil 4 small heatproof ramekins or cups. For the caramel sauce, bring the sugar and cold water to a boil in a small saucepan. Let it boil for a few minutes, until the syrup starts to turn a caramel color. Remove from the heat and stir in 1 tablespoon of hot water. Pour the sauce into the ramekins. Cool, then refrigerate so the sauce sets.

Break the eggs into a small mixing bowl. Split open the vanilla bean with a knife and scrape out the seeds. Place the vanilla bean in a saucepan with the milk. Add the sugar and heat on medium heat until just under the boiling point. Take the pan off the heat. Pour the milk very gradually over the eggs, stirring all the time. Strain the custard, then pour into the ramekins.

Bring a large pan of water to a boil. Place the ramekins in a steamer basket and set over the boiling water. Reduce the heat to low, cover the steamer basket and cook for about 10 to 11 minutes, or until the custard is just set. Take off the heat and let the crèmes cool in the covered steamer basket for 10 minutes, then refrigerate again until chilled. Just before serving, run a sharp knife around the edge of each ramekin. Place a plate on top and carefully turn over to unmold the crème.

COFFEE ROLL CAKE
ロールケーキ

SERVES 8
30 MINS PREPARATION TIME
11 MINS COOKING TIME

3 eggs, separated
50 g (1¾ oz) sugar
50 g (1¾ oz) cake flour
  or all-purpose flour
2 tablespoons instant
  coffee + 2 tablespoons
  hot water

Cream and decoration
200ml (7 fl oz)
  whipping cream
1 tablespoon
  instant coffee
1 tablespoon
  coffee liqueur
2 tablespoons sugar
3 tablespoons
  flaked almonds
chocolate shavings

Line a 27 cm (10¾ in) square baking pan or sheet with parchment paper and preheat the oven to 180°C (350°F). With an electric mixer, beat the egg yolks and 40 g (1½ oz) of the sugar on medium speed until pale and light. Sift in half of the flour and fold in using a spatula. Dissolve the coffee in the hot water and add to the batter, along with the rest of the flour. Fold with the spatula until the flour is well incorporated. Put the egg whites and the remaining 10 g (¼ oz) of sugar into another bowl and whip to firm peaks. Add a third of the egg-white mixture to the cake batter and fold in gently. Repeat this process with the rest of the egg-white mixture, using a spatula to scrape the bottom of the bowl and being careful to keep as much air as possible in the mixture. When the batter is a uniform color (you can't see any more white), pour the batter into the prepared pan from a height, then smooth the surface.

Lift the pan a couple of centimeters (an inch) from the work surface and let it drop to eliminate air bubbles. Bake the cake for 11 minutes, then check if it is done by gently pressing with your finger—if the cake springs back, it is done. Remove from the oven, cover with foil and leave to cool. Turn out the cake with its parchment paper, then carefully peel off the paper, saving it to help with rolling the cake.

Place some ice cubes in a large bowl. In another bowl, combine the cream, coffee, coffee liqueur and sugar. Put this bowl inside the bowl of ice and whip the cream mixture to firm peaks. Using a spatula, spread half the cream on the cake, putting less cream on the edge of the cake farthest away from you. Firmly roll up the cake by lifting up the parchment paper. Wrap the roll cake in plastic wrap and place in the refrigerator for 1 hour to set the shape. Take out and spread the rest of the cream over the outside of the cake. Draw wavy lines in the cream with a fork and press on the flaked almonds. Decorate with chocolate shavings.

SHORTCAKE

JAPANESE STRAWBERRY SHORTCAKE
ショートケーキ

SERVES 6
40 MINS PREPARATION TIME
35–40 MINS COOKING TIME

80 g (2¾ oz) cake flour or
   all-purpose flour
½ teaspoon baking powder
3 eggs
80 g (2¾ oz) white sugar
1 tablespoon milk
20 g (¾ oz) butter, melted

Syrup
100 ml (3½ fl oz) water
50 g (1¾ oz) white sugar
1 tablespoon kirsch

Filling
300 ml (10½ fl oz)
   whipping cream
30 g (1 oz) sugar
300 g (10½ oz) strawberries

Preheat the oven to 160°C (315°F) and line an 18 cm (7 in) round cake pan with parchment paper. Sift together the flour and baking powder. Using an electric mixer, beat the eggs for 30 seconds on low speed. Add half of the sugar and beat for another 30 seconds. Add the rest of the sugar, increase the speed to medium and beat for about 3 minutes, then increase the speed to maximum and beat for 2 minutes. The batter should be light and creamy. Whisk with a hand whisk for 2 minutes, then add half of the flour mixture and gently fold it in using a spatula. Add the rest of the flour and fold in the same way until the flour is well incorporated (be careful not to collapse the air in the mixture). Stir the milk into the melted butter, then gradually add this in a thin stream, folding it in. Pour the batter into the pan. Lift the pan a couple of centimeters (an inch) from the work surface and let it drop to eliminate air bubbles. Bake for 30 to 35 minutes.

Once the cake is cooked, drop the pan twice more to knock out some of the air. Turn out immediately and cool on a rack. When the cake is cool, cut it in half horizontally.

To make the syrup, place the water and sugar in a small saucepan on medium heat. When the sugar has completely dissolved, turn off the heat, add the kirsch and leave to cool. For the filling, place some ice cubes in a large bowl. Put the cream and sugar in another bowl and place it inside the bowl of ice, then whip to soft peaks. Set aside 8 whole strawberries and cut the rest into 6 mm (¼ in) slices. Brush two-thirds of the syrup on the two cut sides of the cake. Spread 5–6 tablespoons of cream on one of the cake halves and arrange the sliced strawberries on top. Cover with another 4 tablespoons of whipped cream, then put the other cake half on top. Brush the surface of the cake with syrup, then cover the top and sides with more of the cream. Whip the rest of the cream again to make it firmer. Place the cream in a piping bag, decorate the outside of the cake and arrange the whole strawberries on top. Chill the cake to set the cream.

CHIFFON CAKE

シフォンケーキ

MAKES 1 CAKE

20 MINS PREPARATION TIME

30 MINS COOKING TIME

4 eggs, separated
90 g (3¼ oz) caster
  (superfine) sugar
60 ml (2 fl oz/¼ cup) milk

55 ml (1¾ fl oz) sunflower oil
70 g (2½ oz) cake flour or
  all-purpose flour

Preheat the oven to 180°C (350°F). Whisk the egg yolks and 30 g (1 oz) of the sugar until pale and frothy. Gradually add the milk, whisking constantly. Add the oil in the same way. Sift in the flour and combine well with a spatula. Using an electric mixer, whisk the egg whites on medium speed until foamy. Add 30 g (1 oz) of the sugar and increase the speed to high. Once the egg whites start to firm up, add the rest of the sugar and keep whisking until the meringue forms stiff peaks. Add a third of the meringue mixture to the egg yolk mixture. Mix well using a hand whisk, lifting the batter from the bottom of the bowl. Repeat the process with another third of the meringue. Gently fold in the last third of the meringue mixture using a spatula, scraping the batter from the bottom of the bowl until the color of the batter is uniform, and being careful to retain as much air as possible.

Pour the batter into a 17 cm (6½ in) chiffon cake pan. (Important: you must not butter or flour the pan!) Bake for about 30 minutes, without opening the oven at any time. To check if the cake is done, insert the tip of a knife—it should come out clean. Remove the pan from the oven, turn it upside down and place it over the neck of a full bottle so it doesn't fall over. This prevents the cake from collapsing. Pass a long thin-bladed knife around the cooled cake and turn it out. Serve with Chantilly cream or vanilla ice cream.

JAPANESE-STYLE CRÊPE CONE
クレープ

MAKES 8

20 MINS PREPARATION TIME + **1 HR** RESTING TIME

2 MINS COOKING TIME PER CRÊPE

2 eggs
20 g (¾ oz) sugar
100 g (3½ oz) cake flour or
   all-purpose flour
15 g (½ oz) unsalted
   butter, melted
250 ml (9 fl oz/1 cup) milk

sunflower oil

Chantilly cream
300 ml (10½ fl oz)
   whipping cream

15 g (½ oz) caster
   (superfine) sugar

Fillings
8 strawberries,
   cut into quarters
8 scoops vanilla ice cream
16 chocolate cigarettes
   russes (rolled wafer cookies)
8 tablespoons
   blueberry jam

Place the eggs and sugar in a stainless-steel mixing bowl. Sift in the flour and combine well with a whisk. Add the melted butter, then the milk, whisking constantly. Let the batter rest for at least 1 hour in the refrigerator.

To make the Chantilly cream, whip the cream to soft peaks. Once the cream has thickened, add the sugar and keep whipping until the cream holds firm peaks. Lightly oil the crêpe pan, wiping away any excess with a paper towel. Heat the pan and pour in a small ladleful of batter, spreading it out to make a thin crêpe. Once the edge of the crêpe is cooked and the surface starts to dry out (after about 1 minute), turn the crêpe over and cook for about 1 more minute.

Place a spoonful of the Chantilly cream, 2 strawberries and a scoop of ice cream in a V shape on each crêpe. Fold the crêpe over the filling (so you can still see the ice cream), then roll it into a cone. Decorate with 2 cigarettes russes, 1 tablespoon of blueberry jam and 2 more strawberries. Wrap in paper.

CRÊPES

クレープ

In Tokyo, crêpes have been reinvented in a very colorful style. Filled with a large amount of Chantilly cream, fruit, ice cream and chocolate, they are far from light, but they are very kawaii (cute): girls love them!

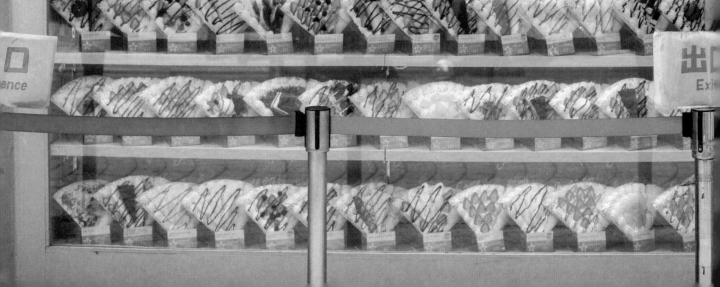

ICE CREAM
アイス

SERVES 4
15 MINS PREPARATION TIME
5 MINS COOKING TIME
3 HRS FREEZING TIME

✳ TSUBUAN
= 粒餡
Adzuki bean
paste.
The beans are
left whole.

BLACK SESAME ICE CREAM
黒胡麻アイス

200 ml (7 fl oz) whipping cream	70 ml (2¼ fl oz) milk
2 egg yolks	40 g (1½ oz) black sesame paste
75 g (⅓ cup) sugar	

Whip the cream in a bowl. Place the egg yolks and sugar in another bowl and whisk until pale and light. Heat the milk and black sesame paste in a saucepan on low to medium heat, stirring constantly. Just before it comes to a boil, remove from the heat and slowly pour into the egg yolk mixture, stirring all the time. Add the cream and mix well. Pour the mixture into an ice cream maker and churn according to the directions. If you don't have an ice cream maker, pour the mixture into a metal container and freeze for 3 hours, scraping the ice cream with a fork every hour to break up the ice crystals.

MATCHA ICE CREAM
抹茶アイス

200 ml (7 fl oz) whipping cream	2 egg yolks
1½ tablespoons matcha (green tea powder)	75 g (⅓ cup) sugar
	100 ml (3½ fl oz) milk

Whip the cream and matcha in a bowl. Place the egg yolks and sugar in another bowl and whisk until pale and light. Heat the milk in a saucepan on low to medium heat. Just before it comes to a boil, remove from the heat and slowly pour into the egg yolk mixture, stirring all the time. Add the cream mixture and mix well. Pour the mixture into an ice cream maker and churn according to the directions. If you don't have an ice cream maker, pour the mixture into a metal container and freeze for 3 hours, scraping the ice cream with a fork every hour to break up the ice crystals.

ADZUKI BEAN ICE CREAM
小豆アイス

200 ml (7 fl oz) whipping cream	75 g (⅓ cup) sugar
2 egg yolks	100 ml (3½ fl oz) milk
	200 g (7 oz) tsubuan*

Whip the cream in a bowl. Place the egg yolks and sugar in another bowl and whisk until pale and light. Heat the milk in a saucepan on low to medium heat. Just before it comes to a boil, remove from the heat and slowly pour into the egg yolk mixture, stirring all the time. Add the cream and tsubuan and mix well. Pour the mixture into an ice cream maker and churn according to the directions. If you don't have an ice cream maker, pour the mixture into a metal container and freeze for 3 hours, scraping the ice cream with a fork every hour to break up the ice crystals.

SORBET
シャーベット

SHISO SORBET

紫蘇シャーベット

SERVES 4
15 MINS PREPARATION TIME
3 MINS COOKING TIME
3 HRS FREEZING TIME

140 g (5 oz) sugar
30 g (1 oz) grated ginger
300 ml (10½ fl oz) water
4 shiso (perilla) leaves
juice of 1 organic lemon
1 tablespoon egg white

Put the sugar, ginger and water in a saucepan. Heat on medium heat until the sugar has completely dissolved. Strain to remove any ginger fibers, then cool to room temperature. Transfer to a blender or food processor, add the shiso leaves, lemon juice and egg white and blend until smooth. Pour the mixture into an ice cream maker and follow the directions for your machine. If you don't have an ice cream maker, pour the mixture into a metal container and freeze for 3 hours, scraping the sorbet with a fork every hour to break up the ice crystals.

Note: For a more granita like texture, make the sorbet manually instead of in an ice cream maker.

YUZU SORBET

柚子シャーベット

SERVES 4
15 MINS PREPARATION TIME
3 MINS COOKING TIME
3 HRS FREEZING TIME

15 g (½ oz) gelatin sheet
100 g (3½ oz) sugar
300 ml (10½ fl oz) water
100 ml (3½ fl oz) yuzu (Japanese citrus fruit) juice
2½ tablespoons umeshu*
50 g (1¾ oz) honey

Soak the gelatin in a bowl of water. Place the sugar and water in a saucepan. Heat on medium heat until the sugar has completely dissolved. Remove from the heat and add the squeezed-out gelatin, yuzu juice, umeshu and honey. Let the mixture cool to room temperature, then pour into an ice cream maker and follow the directions for your machine. If you don't have an ice cream maker, pour the mixture into a metal container and freeze for 3 hours, scraping the sorbet with a fork every hour to break up the ice crystals.

Note: For a more granita like texture, make the sorbet manually instead of in an ice cream maker.

* UMESHU
= 梅酒
plum
liqueur

you eat the plum
after finishing the
drink

SWEET POTATOES

SWEET POTATO CAKES
スゥイートポテト

MAKES 8–IO CAKES
2O MINS PREPARATION TIME
35 MINS COOKING TIME

400 g (14 oz) white sweet potato
40 g (1½ oz) lightly salted butter
50 g (1¾ oz) sugar
2 tablespoons evaporated milk
30 ml (1 fl oz) whipping cream + 1 tablespoon extra
1 egg yolk

Cook the sweet potato whole in a saucepan of boiling water until it is completely cooked and tender in the middle, about 20 minutes. Remove the sweet potato and peel. Chop it roughly and place in a bowl with the butter. Use a stick blender to mash it into a paste. Add the sugar, evaporated milk, whipping cream and half of the egg yolk (saving the other half for the next step). Mix together with a spatula until smooth.

Preheat the oven to 200°C (400°F) and line a baking sheet with parchment paper. Mix the reserved half of the egg yolk with the extra tablespoon of cream to make a glaze. Shape the sweet potato mixture into 10 cm (4 in) long "boats", as in the photo. Place on the prepared baking sheet and brush with the glaze. Bake for about 10 minutes or until the sweet potato cakes are a lovely golden brown.

KABOCHA CHAKIN-SHIBORI

TWISTED PUMPKIN BALLS

南瓜茶巾絞り

MAKES 8
15 MINS PREPARATION TIME
5 MINS COOKING TIME

300 g (10½ oz) pumpkin
4 tablespoons water
1 tablespoon sunflower oil
2 tablespoons crème de marrons de l'Ardèche
  (sweetened chestnut purée)
1 tablespoon raw (demerara) sugar
1 tablespoon matcha (green tea powder)

Peel and seed the pumpkin, then cut into 2 cm (¾ in) cubes. Place the pumpkin, water and oil in a saucepan with a lid. Cook on low heat for about 5 minutes until the pumpkin is completely cooked. Mash the pumpkin well with a fork, then mix in the chestnut purée and sugar. Take out a fifth of the pumpkin mixture and combine with the matcha powder.

Take an eighth of the rest of the pumpkin mixture and put it in the middle of a 15 cm (6 in) square of plastic wrap. Place a rounded teaspoon of the matcha-flavored pumpkin mixture on top. Use the plastic wrap to help you shape the mixture into a ball in the palm of your hand, twisting the wrap tightly. Remove the plastic wrap. Make 7 more balls in the same way.

GYUNYU PURIN
MILK PUDDINGS
牛乳プリン

PUDDINGS

MAKES 4 SMALL GLASSES
10 MINS PREPARATION TIME
3 MINS COOKING TIME

5 g (⅛ oz) powdered gelatin + 2 tablespoons water
350 ml (12 fl oz) whole milk—organic, if possible
3 tablespoons raw (demerara) sugar

Combine the gelatin and water in a small bowl and set aside. Heat the milk and sugar on low heat in a saucepan, stirring to dissolve the sugar. Just before it comes to a boil, remove from the heat, add the gelatin and stir to dissolve completely. Pour the mixture into your chosen glasses. (This quantity is enough for small glasses—if you would like to make larger puddings, double the quantities of ingredients and use larger glasses.) Let the puddings cool to room temperature, then refrigerate for 30 minutes to set.

BLACK SUGAR SAUCE

2 MINS PREPARATION TIME
3 MINS COOKING TIME

50 g (1¾ oz) muscovado (dark brown) sugar
20 g (¾ oz) raw (demerara) sugar
2½ tablespoons water
1 tablespoon honey
2 thin slices ginger, very finely shredded

Place both sugars and the water in a small saucepan on low heat. Once the sugars have completely dissolved, remove from the heat and add the honey. Let the mixture cool completely. Spoon 1 tablespoon of sauce into each glass. Sprinkle with a little shredded ginger.

GINGER–LEMON SAUCE

3 MINS PREPARATION TIME
5 MINS COOKING TIME

50 g (1¾ oz) raw (demerara) sugar
100 ml (3½ fl oz) water
½ organic lemon, cut into into 5 mm (¼ in) slices
10 very thin slices ginger + 4 extra slices

Place all the ingredients except the extra ginger in a saucepan. Cook for 5 minutes on low to medium heat until the sauce is thick. Take off the heat and allow to cool. Spoon 1 tablespoon of sauce into each glass, then decorate with a slice of ginger.

MACERATED BLUEBERRIES

3 MINS PREPARATION TIME

20 blueberries
1 tablespoon raw (demerara) sugar
1 tablespoon kirsch
a few mint leaves

Marinate the blueberries with the sugar and kirsch for 5 minutes. Arrange some blueberries in each glass with the juice and decorate with the mint leaves.

Note: You can make this recipe using different seasonal fruits: strawberries, figs, melon...

飴屋 CONFECTIONERY

A few store owners carry on the traditions of Japanese confectionery. My favorites are the cylindrical sweets called kintaro ame. When they are sliced, the face of Kintaro, a legendary boy hero, appears. For a child, it is magic! I do not know exactly how these sweets are made, but apparently the face is drawn using several tubes, forming a very large sausage. The sausage is then stretched into a thin cylinder.

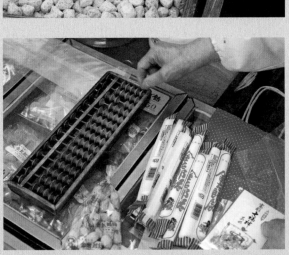

居酒屋

IZAKAYA

TAPAS BAR

Izakaya are bars where you can get something to eat.
Japanese people like to go there in the evenings after
a long day at work. Everyone can find something to
their liking in the variety of dishes offered. Fish, meat,
salads, soups and rice: many of the dishes are salty or
fried, and are served in small quantities like tapas, to be
enjoyed with beer, sake (rice wine), shochu (Japanese
distilled liquor) and wine. These are the dishes I invite
you to discover.

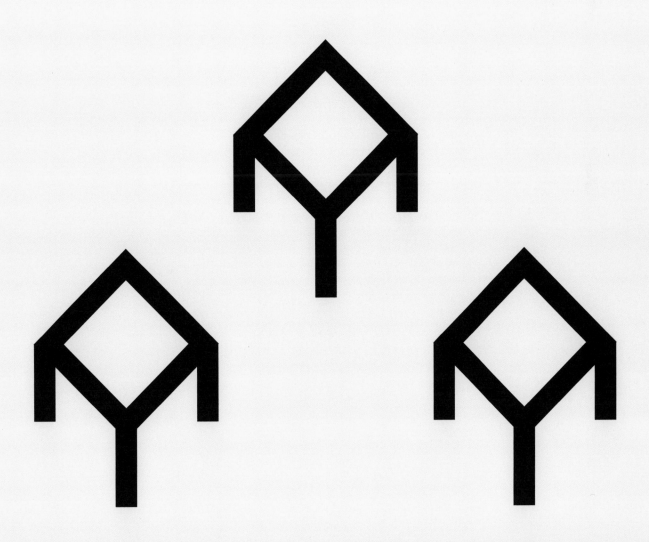

EDAMAME
GREEN SOY BEANS
枝豆

SERVES 4

1 MIN PREPARATION TIME
ABOUT 5 MINS COOKING TIME

3 pinches coarse salt
4 handfuls frozen edamame*
  (soy beans in pods, available from Asian supermarkets)

Bring a saucepan of water to a boil with 2 pinches of the salt. Add the edamame and cook for about 5 to 6 minutes (depending on the time given on the package). Drain and serve in a bowl. Sprinkle with the remaining pinch of salt. This very easy dish is perfect to serve with drinks and is one of the most popular dishes in izakaya. Most of the time, edamame are eaten with alcohol (they go particularly well with beer).

Note: To eat, squeeze the pod so the beans pop out and just eat the beans. Don't forget to put out another empty bowl alongside for the discarded pods.

＊ EDAMAME

= 枝豆   You just eat the beans!

AGEDASHI-DOFU
FRIED TOFU WITH DASHI
揚げ出し豆腐

SERVES 4

20 MINS PREPARATION TIME + **30 MINS** RESTING TIME

4 MINS COOKING TIME

250 g (9 oz) momen tofu
50 g (1¾ oz) all-purpose
  flour
sunflower oil, for frying
2 cm (¾ in) white
  radish (daikon),* grated
2 cm (¾ in) ginger, grated
1 spring onion (scallion),
  thinly sliced on the diagonal

Sauce
200 ml (7 fl oz) dashi
  (see p. 12)
40 ml (1¼ fl oz) mirin
25 ml (¾ fl oz) soy sauce
1 teaspoon potato starch
1 tablespoon water

Wrap the tofu in 2 layers of paper towels. Put a plate on top and leave it to drain for 30 minutes.

To make the sauce, put the dashi, mirin and soy sauce in a saucepan on medium heat. When the sauce boils, reduce the heat to low. In a small bowl, mix the potato starch with the water to make a smooth paste. Add to the sauce and keep stirring until it thickens, then remove from the heat.

Cut the drained tofu into 4 square pieces. Pat dry with a paper towel and then flour the tofu. Heat a 2 cm (¾ in) depth of oil in a high-sided frying pan on medium heat. Cook the tofu on both sides until golden brown, about 3 to 4 minutes. Transfer to a serving dish, then pour over the hot sauce. Garnish with the radish, ginger and slices of spring onion.

✳ WHITE RADISH
= (DAIKON) 大根

You can use black radish as a substitute, but daikon is much larger and milder.

142

AGE HARUMAKI
SPRING ROLLS
揚げ春巻き

MAKES 8 ROLLS (SERVES 4)
20 MINS PREPARATION TIME
5 MINS COOKING TIME

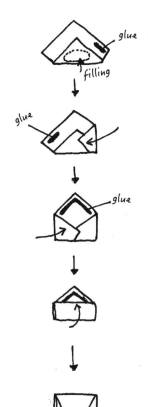

Sauce
4 tablespoons rice vinegar
3 tablespoons soy sauce

16 large raw prawns (shrimp)
1 tablespoon sake
1 teaspoon sesame oil
freshly ground pepper
3 green asparagus spears

1 teaspoon oyster sauce
1 tablespoon all-purpose
   flour
1 tablespoon water
8 spring roll wrappers
3 cm (1¼ in) leek, thinly sliced
2 cm (¾ in) ginger,
   cut into thin matchsticks
sunflower oil, for frying

To make the sauce, combine the vinegar and soy sauce in a small bowl. Set aside.

Peel the prawns, then wipe them dry and marinate in the combined sake, sesame oil and pepper for 10 minutes. Peel the asparagus and cut into 6 mm (¼ in) slices on the diagonal, then combine with the oyster sauce. Blend the flour and water together in a bowl to make a glue to seal the spring rolls. Place a wrapper on the surface, with a corner facing you. Place 2 prawns and 3–4 slices of asparagus horizontally on the wrapper (slightly below the midline) and top with some leek and ginger. Pick up the corner of the wrapper nearest to you and roll up, tucking in the sides and sealing the ends with the flour and water glue. Pour a 3 cm (1¼ in) depth of oil into a flat-bottomed wok or high-sided frying pan and heat to 170°C (325°F). Fry the rolls in a single layer (cook them in batches, if necessary), turning occasionally. Drain and eat immediately with the sauce.

MACARONI SALAD
マカロニサラダ

SERVES 2
20 MINS PREPARATION TIME
ABOUT 10 MINS COOKING TIME

100 g (3½ oz) dried macaroni
80 g (2¾ oz) can of tuna in vegetable oil
4 tablespoons mayonnaise
salt and freshly ground pepper
½ cucumber, very thinly sliced
¼ onion, very finely chopped
½ slice of ham, cut into matchsticks

Cook the macaroni according to the instructions on the package, then drain and leave to cool. Drain the tuna and flake with a fork. Combine the tuna with the mayonnaise and season with salt and pepper. Mix the cucumber with a pinch of salt and set aside for 5 minutes, then squeeze out the excess liquid with your hands. Soak the onion in a bowl of water for 5 minutes to soften its flavor, then drain well. Mix all the ingredients together thoroughly before serving.

SAKE CHAZUKE
RICE WITH GREEN TEA AND GRILLED SALMON
鮭茶漬け

SERVES 4

10 MINS PREPARATION TIME + **OVERNIGHT** RESTING
10 MINS COOKING TIME

2 salmon fillets
1 tablespoon coarse natural salt
4 bowls of cooked rice (see p. 10)
2 tablespoons grated white radish (daikon)
wasabi, to taste
1 sheet of nori, shredded
2–3 tablespoons green tea, infused for 2 to 3 minutes
   in 300 ml (10½ fl oz) boiling water
   (or dashi, see p. 12) in a large teapot

Salt the fillets on both sides, cover with plastic wrap and marinate in the refrigerator overnight. The next day, take out the fillets and sear them on a wire grill rack or chargrill pan (or cook for about 10 minutes in a preheated 180°C/350°F oven). Flake the salmon and season with more salt if necessary—the salmon needs to be fairly salty for this dish.

Place some cooked rice, ideally lukewarm, in four small bowls. If you are using rice that has been in the refrigerator, put it in a colander and rinse gently with hot water to separate the grains, or briefly reheat in the microwave—the aim is to avoid the hard, unpleasant texture of cold rice. Arrange the salmon, white radish, wasabi and nori on the rice. Make the tea (if you have some dashi, you can use it to infuse the tea for extra flavor), then pour the hot tea over the rice and eat straightaway.

NIKU CHAZUKE
RICE WITH TEA AND SIMMERED BEEF
肉茶漬け

SERVES 4
15 MINS PREPARATION TIME
15 MINS COOKING TIME

Shigureni beef
2 teaspoons toasted
   sesame oil
250 g (9 oz) lean
   beef, thinly sliced
4 tablespoons sake
4 tablespoons soy sauce
2 tablespoons mirin
3 teaspoons raw
   (demerara) sugar
1 small handful
   katsuobushi
   (dried bonito flakes)

4 bowls of cooked
   rice (see p. 10)
2 cm (¾ in) ginger,
   finely shredded
1 spring onion (scallion),
   finely chopped
2–3 tablespoons hojicha
   tea (a roasted green tea
   that is brown-colored
   and low in caffeine),
   infused for 2 to 3 minutes
   in 300 ml (10½ fl oz)
   boiling water

For the beef, heat the sesame oil in a small saucepan on low to medium heat and sauté each slice of beef separately (so they don't stick). Return all the beef to the pan and add the remaining ingredients. Stir on medium heat until all of the liquid has evaporated, then remove from the heat. This will keep in the refrigerator for 1 week.

Place some cooked rice, ideally lukewarm, in four small bowls. If you are using rice that has been in the refrigerator, put it in a colander and rinse gently with hot water to separate the grains, or reheat in the microwave—the aim is to avoid the hard, unpleasant texture of cold rice. Top with the shigureni beef, some shredded ginger and chopped spring onion. Make the tea, then pour it over the rice and serve immediately.

KARA-AGE
FRIED CHICKEN
唐揚げ

SERVES 4

10 MINS PREPARATION TIME + AT LEAST **30 MINS** MARINATING TIME
6 MINS COOKING TIME

500 g (1 lb 2 oz)
  boneless chicken
  breast or thigh

oil, for deep-frying
1 organic lemon

Marinade
1 egg
1 garlic clove, grated
2 cm (¾ in) ginger, grated
1 tablespoon sesame oil
1½ tablespoons soy sauce
1 teaspoon raw
  (demerara) sugar
5 tablespoons potato starch
1 teaspoon cinnamon
freshly ground pepper

Cut the chicken into 4 cm (1½ in) pieces. Combine all the marinade ingredients in a bowl, add the chicken and mix well. Leave to marinate in the refrigerator for at least 30 minutes (or overnight). Stir the marinade and chicken again well before frying, as the potato starch tends to settle on the bottom of the bowl. Pour a 5 cm (2 in) depth of oil into a large saucepan and heat to 170°C (325°F) on medium to high heat. Carefully add the chicken pieces with their marinade and cook for about 5 to 6 minutes, turning regularly, until nicely browned and cooked through. To test, pierce a piece of chicken with a fork: if the juice comes out clear, it is cooked. Remove the chicken from the oil and drain on paper towels. Squeeze some lemon juice over and serve immediately.

ASARI NO SAKAMUSHI

SAKE-STEAMED CLAMS

浅蜊の酒蒸し

SERVES 4

10 MINS PREPARATION TIME + **1 HR–OVERNIGHT** RESTING TIME

3 MINS COOKING TIME

1 kg (2 lb 4 oz) very fresh clams
1 tablespoon salt
2 tablespoons sunflower oil
1 garlic clove, finely chopped
150 ml (5 fl oz) sake
1 teaspoon soy sauce
2–3 spring onions (scallions), thinly silced

Place the clams in a large bowl of water with the salt and set aside for 1 hour (or overnight in the refrigerator), so the clams "spit out" any sand. Next, rinse the clams, rubbing them together to clean their shells. Drain. In a deep frying pan with a lid, start heating the oil with the garlic. Add the clams and the sake, then cover and cook on high heat for 2 to 3 minutes or until all the clams have opened. Be careful not to overcook them. Stir in the soy sauce and sprinkle with the spring onions, then remove from the heat and serve.

HOTATE SALAD
WHITE RADISH AND SCALLOP SALAD
ホタテと大根のサラダ

SERVES 4
15 MINS PREPARATION TIME
5–10 MINS COOKING TIME

10 cm (4 in) white
  radish (daikon)
1 teaspoon fine natural salt
200 g (7 oz) scallops
1 tablespoon sake
1 teaspoon soy sauce

4 tablespoons mayonnaise
juice of ¼ organic lemon
1 chive, finely chopped
freshly ground pepper
chive flowers—optional

Peel the white radish and slice into 2 mm (1/16 in) rounds, then into very thin matchsticks. Combine with the salt in a bowl and leave to marinate for 10 minutes. Drain, squeezing well with your hands. Place the scallops on a plate and pour the sake over. Cover with plastic wrap and cook in the microwave oven for about 3 minutes at 600 watts. Turn the scallops over and cook for another 2 minutes. Check that the scallops are cooked through. If you do not have a microwave, steam the scallops on a plate (so you don't lose the juices) for 10 minutes on medium to high heat. Save the juices (very important!) and break the cooked scallops into small pieces with your hands. Combine the radish, soy sauce, mayonnaise, lemon juice and chives with the scallops and their reserved juices. Season with pepper and arrange on a plate with a few chive flowers, if you have them.

✳ WHITE RADISH
  (DAIKON)

= 大根
cousin of the
black radish,
but much
larger and
milder

MAGURO NO TARUTARU

TUNA TARTARE

マグロのタルタル

SERVES 4

10 MINS PREPARATION TIME

400 g (14 oz) sashimi-grade tuna fillet

1 rounded teaspoon pine nuts
1 teaspoon sesame seeds
1 teaspoon sunflower seeds
1 small pinch coarse natural salt
dill and baby shiso (perilla)—optional

Marinade
1 garlic clove
1 tablespoon sake
1 tablespoon miso
1 tablespoon soy sauce
2 tablespoons raw (demerara) sugar
2 tablespoons rice vinegar
2 tablespoons toasted sesame oil
½ sheet nori, torn into small pieces

Finely dice the tuna. Combine all the marinade ingredients in a bowl and add the tuna. Mix together the pine nuts, sesame seeds and sunflower seeds, then add half to the tuna and mix well. Arrange the tuna on a plate. Scatter the rest of the pine nut and seed mixture over it, then sprinkle with a pinch of salt and the herbs, if using.

FUROFUKI DAIKON

SIMMERED WHITE RADISH
ふろふき大根

SERVES 4
20 MINS PREPARATION TIME
50 MINS COOKING TIME

⅓ – ½ white radish
  (daikon), depending on size
10 cm x 10 cm (4 in x 4 in)
  piece kombu seaweed

yuzu zest

Sauce
4 tablespoons miso
4 tablespoons mirin
1 tablespoon raw
  (demerara) sugar
1 tablespoon sake
1 teaspoon soy sauce
1 tablespoon yuzu juice

Slice the white radish into 3 cm (1¼ in) thick rounds. Peel the slices and trim the sharp edges of the rounds so they don't break up during cooking. Score a cross in each side of the rounds to help them cook more evenly. Place the kombu in the base of a wide saucepan and then lay the radish rounds on top in a single layer. Cover with water and bring to a boil, then reduce the heat to medium and simmer for 40 minutes. Place all the sauce ingredients in a small saucepan on medium heat and cook, stirring constantly. Once the sauce is very hot, reduce the heat and cook on very low heat for 5 minutes, still stirring. Place the kombu and radish rounds in a bowl, then pour a little of the cooking liquid over. Spoon some miso sauce onto each piece of radish, then garnish with yuzu zest.

Note: Bergamot zest will also work very well in place of the yuzu zest.

YUZU
柚子

Its zest adds
fragrance
to dishes.

陶器 CERAMICS

Almost all of the ceramics you see in this book were made by Japanese artisans. Their art is passed down from generation to generation, with the clay, decorations and color varying from region to region. In comparison, mass-produced ceramics lack softness and character.

TAKO NO KARA AGE
FRIED OCTOPUS WITH BUTTERNUT SQUASH
蛸の唐揚げ

SERVES 4

15 MINS PREPARATION TIME + **15–20 MINS** MARINATING TIME
20 MINS COOKING TIME

400 g (14 oz) boiled octopus

3 tablespoons potato starch
200 g (7 oz) butternut
  squash
vegetable oil, for frying
chopped spring
  onion (scallion)
Sichuan pepper

coarse natural salt
¼ organic lime

Marinade
2 tablespoons soy sauce
1 tablespoon sake
½ garlic clove, grated
1 teaspoon grated ginger

Cut the octopus body into 3 cm (1¼ in) pieces and the tentacles into 5 cm (2 in) lengths. Combine all the marinade ingredients in a bowl, add the octopus and leave to marinate for 15 to 20 minutes. Drain and dry well (especially the tentacles) with paper towels, so the oil doesn't spatter during cooking. Place the octopus and potato starch in a plastic bag, then close the bag and shake to coat all the octopus pieces. Peel the butternut squash, remove the seeds and cut into slices about 4 cm (1½ in) long and 1 cm (½ in) thick. Pour a 4 cm (1½ in) depth of oil in a frying pan and heat to about 170°C (325°F). Start by frying the squash until tender. Once the pieces of squash are cooked, drain them on paper towels. Next, fry the octopus until golden and crisp. Serve the squash and octopus sprinkled with spring onion, Sichuan pepper, salt and lime juice.

ODEN
JAPANESE WINTER STEW
おでん

SERVES 4
30 MINS PREPARATION TIME
55 MINS COOKING TIME

12 cm (4½ in) white radish (daikon)

1 block (about 220 g/7¾ oz) konnyaku

2 blocks (about 200 g/7 oz) atsu-age (fried tofu)

2 packages (about 200 g/7 oz) hanpen*

4 packages (about 150 g/5½ oz) satsuma age**

4 potatoes

4 hard-boiled eggs

karashi***

Stock

1.5 liters (52 fl oz/6 cups) dashi (see p. 12)

4 tablespoons soy sauce

4 tablespoons mirin

1 teaspoon salt

Slice the white radish into 3 cm (1¼ in) thick rounds. Peel the slices and trim the sharp edges of the rounds so they don't break up during cooking. Score a cross in each side of the rounds to help them cook more evenly. Cook in a pan of simmering water for 20 minutes, then drain. Cut the konnyaku in half on the diagonal, then lightly score the surface in a cross-hatch pattern so it will absorb the flavors of the stock as it cooks. Cut the blocks of atsu-age and hanpen in half on the diagonal, and unwrap the satsuma age. Peel the potatoes, then cook in a pot of simmering water for 15 minutes. Peel the eggs. Place the stock ingredients in a large saucepan or donabe (a large Japanese earthenware pot—if you have one of these, you can serve the oden from it at the table). Add all the prepared ingredients and bring to a boil. Reduce the heat to low, cover and simmer for 40 minutes. Serve the oden in bowls with Japanese mustard.

* HANPEN

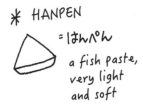

= はんぺん
a fish paste, very light and soft

** SATSUMA AGE

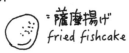

= 薩摩揚げ
fried fishcake

** KARASHI

= 辛子
Japanese mustard, much stronger than French mustard

AJINO NAMEROU
HORSE MACKEREL TARTARE
鯵のなめろう

SERVES 4
10 MINS PREPARATION TIME

2 x 185 g (6½ oz) sashimi-grade Japanese horse mackerel
4 shiso (perilla) or cilantro leaves
2 cm (¾ in) ginger, peeled
3 chives
1 rounded tablespoon miso
1 teaspoon soy sauce
1 teaspoon extra-virgin olive oil

Garnish
4 shiso* (perilla) leaves

Ask the fishmonger to fillet the horse mackerel. Remove the skin. Cut the fillets in half lengthwise, then remove the bones and thinly slice the fish. Shred the herb leaves. Chop the ginger and chives. Place the fish, herbs, ginger, chives and miso on a chopping board. Using a large knife, chop everything together to produce a tartare texture. Combine the horse mackerel tartare with the soy sauce and olive oil in a bowl. Lay a shiso leaf on each plate and divide the horse mackerel tartare among them.

Note: You can replace the horse mackerel with sardines. This is a Japanese fisherman's recipe, prepared on the boat. Enjoy with fresh Karakuchi (dry) sake, beer or a robust dry white wine.

✳ SHISO
紫蘇 Perilla frutescens
this very aromatic
herb is popular in
Japan

GRILLED SHIITAKES
焼き椎茸

SERVES 4
5 MINS PREPARATION TIME
10 MINS COOKING TIME

juice of ½ organic lemon, or your choice of citrus fruit—
  yuzu if you have it, or bergamot, or even lime
1 tablespoon soy sauce
10 fresh shiitake mushrooms
coarse natural salt
3 cm (1¼ in) white radish (daikon), grated

Combine the citrus juice with the soy sauce in a small bowl
to make a sauce. Set aside.

Clean the shiitakes by brushing gently (you should never wash
them), then remove the stems. Heat a chargrill pan or frying pan
on low heat. Place the shiitakes in the pan, gill side upward, and
cook for 7 minutes, without turning them.

Arrange the grilled shiitakes on a plate and sprinkle lightly with
salt. Add the grated radish to the plate and pour the sauce over.
Eat a shiitake first by itself and then with the radish.

ASPARAGUS
IN DASHI
浸しアスパラガス

SERVES 4–6
15 MINS PREPARATION TIME
4 MINS COOKING TIME
1 HR RESTING TIME

Marinade
400–600 ml (14–21 fl oz) dashi (see p. 12)
1 pinch unrefined salt
1 teaspoon soy sauce
1 tablespoon mirin

1 bunch green asparagus
1 teaspoon salt
extra-virgin olive oil, for drizzling

To make the marinade, mix together the dashi, salt, soy sauce and mirin. Choose a container with a lid that will hold the asparagus whole (you could also cut them down to size, but it's nice to serve them whole). Wash the asparagus. Cut off the tough base of each spear, then peel the lower part. Cook in boiling salted water for 3 to 4 minutes (the asparagus needs to stay slightly crisp). Cool the asparagus in iced water to preserve their lovely green color, then drain on paper towels. Place the asparagus in the container and pour in enough marinade to completely cover them. Leave to marinate for at least 1 hour. Arrange the asparagus in a deep plate and pour all the marinade over them. Finish with a drizzle of olive oil.

TEBA SHICHIMI

CHICKEN WINGS WITH SALT AND SHICHIMI

手羽七味

SERVES 4

10 MINS PREPARATION TIME + **1 HR** MARINATING TIME

7 MINS COOKING TIME

500 g (1 lb 2 oz) chicken wings
1 tablespoon coarse natural salt
1 garlic clove, grated
2 tablespoons sake
½ organic lime
shichimi*

Combine the chicken wings with the salt, garlic and sake in a bowl, working it into the meat with your hands. Cover and leave to marinate in a cool place for at least 1 hour. If it will be more than an hour before you cook the chicken, put it in the refrigerator. Cut the wings in 2 at the joint. Heat a frying pan on medium heat and when it is hot, cook the wings on both sides until golden brown, about 7 minutes.

Arrange the chicken wings on a plate. Sprinkle with lime juice, shichimi and, if you like, salt. Serve immediately—these are even better with beer!

＊ SHICHIMI

= 七味
Japanese spice mix
with 7 ingredients

mandarin zest

sesame seeds

hemp
seeds

sansho
pepper

poppy
seeds

aonori

red chili

TOFU
SALAD
豆腐サラダ

SERVES 4
15 MINS PREPARATION TIME
1 MIN COOKING TIME

Dressing
3 tablespoons toasted sesame oil
3 tablespoons soy sauce
1 tablespoon rice vinegar
1 small garlic clove, grated
1 cm (½ in) ginger, finely chopped

1 package silken tofu (about 350–400 g/10½–14 oz)

Salad
a few salad leaves of your choice, such as
  red oak, arugula, mesclun
2 okra pods
¼ cucumber, cut into thin matchsticks
¼ red onion, very thinly sliced
1 rounded tablespoon peanuts, roughly chopped

Mix together the dressing ingredients and set aside. Take the tofu out of its package and drain. Wash the salad leaves. Cook the okra for 1 minute in boiling salted water, then drain and cut into 5 mm (¼ in) pieces. Arrange the salad leaves on a plate. Place the tofu on the salad leaves, whole or cut in half (depending on the size of the tofu), then top with the okra, cucumber, onion and peanuts. Pour the dressing over at the last minute.

BUTASHABU SALAD

SLICED PORK SALAD

豚しゃぶサラダ

SERVES 4
20 MINS PREPARATION TIME
10 MINS COOKING TIME

300 g (10½ oz) pork,
  thinly sliced

½ bunch shungiku*
  (or you can use
  spinach instead)
2 teaspoons toasted
  sesame oil
1 tablespoon toasted
  sesame seeds
3 cm (1¼ in) leek
  (white part), cut into
  very thin matchsticks

Dressing
4 tablespoons
  soy sauce
3 tablespoons
  rice vinegar
2 tablespoons
  raw (demerara) sugar
2 tablespoons
  toasted sesame oil
2 cm (¾ in) leek
  (white part), finely chopped
2 cm (¾ in) ginger,
  finely chopped
½ garlic clove,
  finely chopped
1 teaspoon tobanjan**

✳ SHUNGIKU

= 春菊
edible
chrysanthemum

you can find
it in Chinese
supermarkets

✳✳ TOBANJAN

= 豆板醤
Chinese fermented
bean and chili paste.
You can substitute
1 teaspoon brown
miso and ½ teaspoon
mild chili flakes.

Bring a saucepan of water to a boil and reduce the heat to as low
as possible (you should barely see any movement on the surface
of the water). Add the sliced pork, making sure the slices don't
stick together. When the meat is cooked (pale all over), remove
from the heat and drain. Mix together all the dressing ingredients.
Pluck the leaves from the shungiku stems, then wash and drain
them well. Mix together the shungiku, sesame oil and sesame
seeds in a bowl. Arrange on a plate. Place the pork on top and
then the leek. Pour the dressing over just before serving.

SEAWEED SALAD
海藻サラダ

SERVES 4

15 MINS PREPARATION TIME

10 g (¼ oz) mixed dried
seaweed: wakame,
hijiki, tenkusa, funori...
you will find these in
Japanese supermarkets,
or use a selection of the
seaweed available from
organic food stores
2 cm (¾ in) white
radish (daikon)
⅛ cucumber

toasted sesame seeds
dill

Dressing
2 tablespoons white
sesame paste
2 tablespoons soy sauce
1 tablespoon raw
(demerara) sugar
2 tablespoons rice vinegar
juice of ⅛ organic lemon
1 cm (½ in) ginger,
finely chopped
2 tablespoons toasted
sesame oil

Place the seaweed in a large bowl of water and let the seaweed
rehydrate according to the instructions on the package. Drain it
well. Peel and slice the white radish into 2 mm (1/16 in) rounds,
then into 3 mm (⅛ in) matchsticks. Cut the cucumber in half
lengthwise, then into 3 mm (⅛ in) slices on the diagonal. Make
the dressing by mixing all the ingredients together. Combine
the seaweed, white radish and cucumber in a bowl. Divide the
mixture among four individual bowls and add the dressing just
before serving. Sprinkle with sesame seeds and dill.

LOTUS ROOT CHIPS
蓮根チップス

SERVES 4

5 MINS PREPARATION TIME + **10–20 MINS** RESTING TIME
10–15 MINS COOKING TIME (TO FRY SEVERAL BATCHES)

10–15 cm (4–6 in) lotus root
1 tablespoon rice vinegar
sunflower oil, for frying
fine natural salt

Peel the lotus root and finely slice using a mandoline. Drop the slices into a large bowl of water with the rice vinegar added and leave to soak for 10 to 20 minutes. (This removes the excess starch to make the chips crisper.) Drain, then place the slices on paper towels and cover with another layer of paper towels to remove as much moisture as possible. Heat a 3 cm (1¼ in) depth of oil in a frying pan to 170°C (325°F). Add the slices of lotus root in a single layer and fry until lightly browned, turning them two or three times. Drain on paper towels, then season with salt and serve.

TSUKUNE
CHICKEN MEATBALLS
つくね

SERVES 4

15 MINS PREPARATION TIME

10 MINS COOKING TIME

Sauce
2½ tablespoons soy sauce
2½ tablespoons mirin
1 tablespoon sugar
1 tablespoon oyster sauce
1 garlic clove, bruised

400 g (14 oz) ground chicken
2 spring onions (scallions),
  finely chopped

2 cm (¾ in) ginger, grated
1 tablespoon soy sauce
1 tablespoon mirin
1 teaspoon sesame oil
⅓ egg

1 teaspoon cornstarch
sunflower oil, for frying

Combine all the sauce ingredients and set aside. Put the chicken, spring onion and ginger in a large bowl and knead them together well until the mixture is smooth and even. Add the rest of the ingredients except the oil and mix well. Roll into small balls about 2 cm (¾ in) in diameter if you want to make yakitori skewers, or shape into larger balls about 4–5 cm (1½–2 in) in diameter, as in the photo. Heat a 2 cm (¾ in) depth of oil in a frying pan. Add the meatballs and cook on medium heat until browned, then turn, cover and leave to cook right through to the center. Add the sauce to the frying pan and cook on high heat until smooth and thick. Coat the meatballs in the sauce, turning them over in the frying pan (be careful, as the sauce can burn quite quickly). Remove the garlic. Serve immediately.

Note: I love to serve tsukune with an egg yolk per person to make a sauce. As it is eaten raw, make sure the egg is ultra-fresh.

YAKITORI
CHICKEN
SKEWERS
焼き鳥

SERVES 4–6
20 MINS PREPARATION TIME
40 MINS COOKING TIME

Yakitori sauce
100 ml (3½ fl oz) soy sauce
100 ml (3½ fl oz) mirin
1 tablespoon sugar
1 tablespoon oyster sauce

2 boneless chicken thighs
100 g (3½ oz) chicken livers
2 tablespoons vinegar
**100 g (3½ oz) chicken
  gizzards**
bamboo or wooden skewers

Place all the yakitori sauce ingredients in a small saucepan. Cook on low heat and reduce by half—be careful, as it burns easily. You can keep the sauce for 3 weeks in the refrigerator. Trim any gristle from the chicken thighs, but don't remove the skin: it is the best part of the yakitori! Cut into pieces about 2 cm x 1.5 cm (¾ in x ⅝ in). Rinse the chicken livers in a bowl of water with the vinegar added. Dry them well and cut into pieces the same size as the chicken thigh pieces. Cut the gizzards in the same way. Thread 4 pieces of chicken thigh onto a skewer, leaving 2 cm (¾ in) at the end so you can hold it. Make skewers from the livers and the gizzards in the same way.

If you have a gas grill or a barbecue, cook the skewers on it, turning them from time to time as they cook. When they are almost done, brush the pieces with the yakitori sauce. Once the chicken is coated, continue cooking the skewers, turning them several times (make sure they don't overcook). If you don't have a grill, use a frying pan that is large enough to hold the skewers (or make them smaller). Add a little oil to the frying pan and cook on medium heat, turning from time to time, in the same way as on the grill. When the chicken is cooked, add the sauce to the frying pan. Wait a little for the sauce to reduce and then turn the chicken over in the sauce to coat (be careful, it is very easy to burn the sauce).

GANMODOKI
TOFU FRITTERS
がんもどき

SERVES 4 (MAKES ABOUT 8 FRITTERS)
25 MINS PREPARATION TIME
7 MINS COOKING TIME

1 block of tofu
  (about 400 g/14 oz)
1 tablespoon dried hijiki*
1 egg yolk
¼ onion, thinly sliced
¼ carrot, cut into
  thin matchsticks

4 tablespoons potato starch
1 pinch salt
1 teaspoon soy sauce
  + extra to serve
sunflower oil, for frying
2 cm (¾ in) ginger, grated

Roughly mash the tofu. Line a colander with a double layer of paper towels, then place the tofu in the colander and leave to drain for 15 minutes. Meanwhile, soak the hijiki in a bowl of water for 5 minutes, then drain. Mash the tofu well with a fork in a bowl. Add the hijiki, egg yolk, onion, carrot, potato starch, salt and soy sauce. Mix again. Lightly oil your hands (to prevent the mixture from sticking to them), then form into balls about 4 cm (1½ in) in diameter. Press them lightly between your hands to flatten a little. If the mixture is difficult to shape, use two large spoons. Pour a 4 cm (1½ in) depth of sunflower oil in a saucepan and heat to 160°C (315°F) on medium heat. Cook the fritters until golden brown on both sides, about 6 to 7 minutes, then drain on paper towels. Serve immediately with a little ginger and soy sauce.

Note: Use the standard momen tofu found in Japanese food stores, or Chinese tofu, for this recipe. Avoid silken tofu here, as it contains too much water. If you can only find the extra-firm tofu in health food stores, skip the draining step.

✳ HIJIKI
= ひじき
A black seaweed, like mini noodles. Very high in minerals.

188

居酒屋

IZAKAYA

TAPAS BAR

Japanese society can be particularly stressful. There are a lot of social rules dictated by one's status, sex and age that create barriers. Around alcohol, we can finally let go and stop paying as much attention to these rules. Bars are thus considered essential by Japanese people!

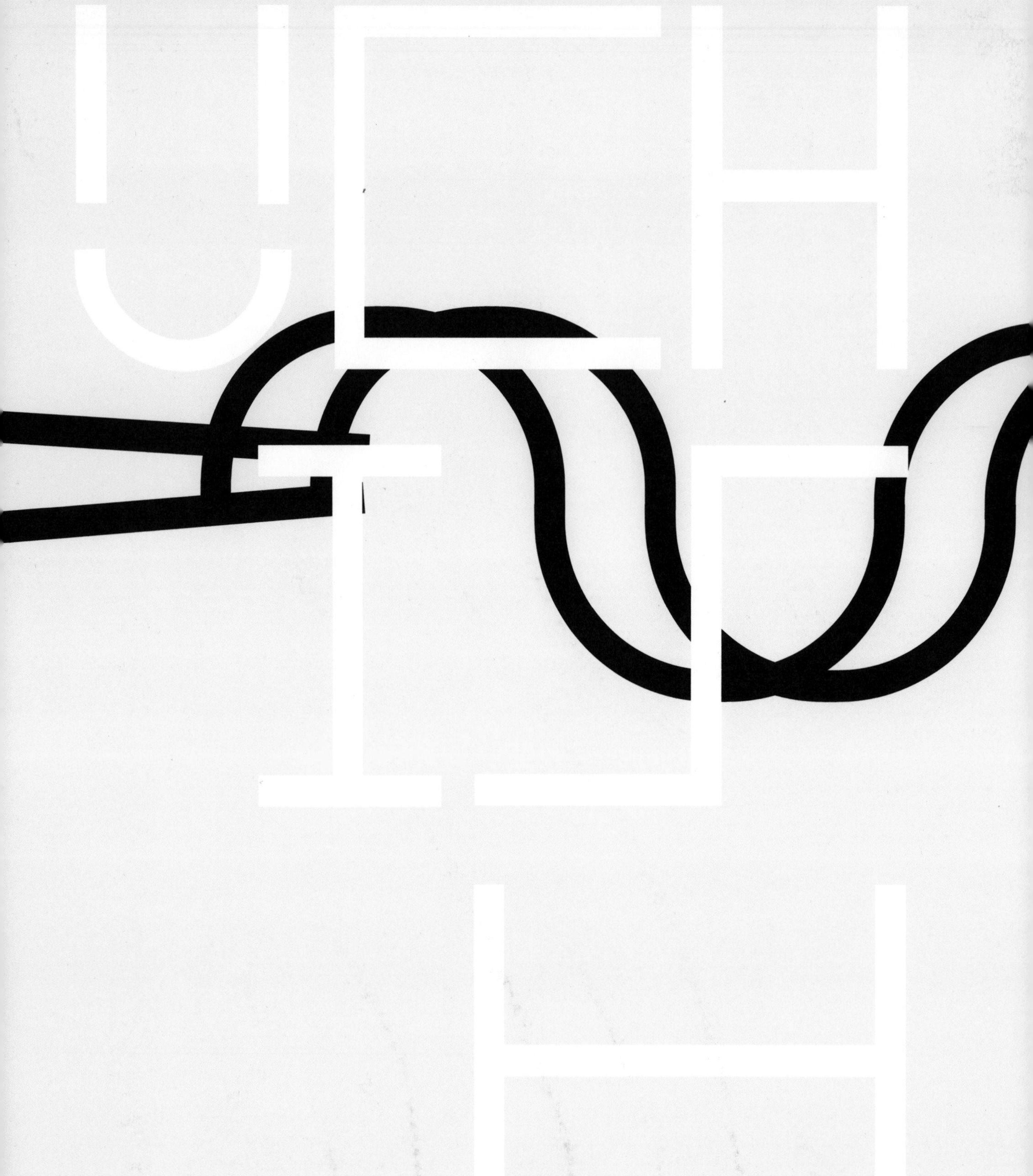

内食

UCHISHOKU

HOME COOKING

For the Japanese, it is important to eat well and as a family. In day-to-day life, families eat salads, simmered or breaded meats, marinated or poached fish, and gather around convivial dishes such as **nabe** (hotpot) or the famous **sushi**, but made home-style.

PAN-FRIED PORK GYOZA

豚と白菜の焼き餃子

SERVES 6 (4–5 GYOZA PER PERSON)
30 MINS PREPARATION TIME
10 MINS COOKING TIME

1 package (about 25–30)
  gyoza wrappers

sunflower and toasted
  sesame oil, for frying
300 ml (10½ fl oz) water

Filling
⅛ Chinese cabbage or
  4 leaves white cabbage
2 teaspoons salt
200 g (7 oz) ground
  pork belly
1 tablespoon soy sauce
1 tablespoon sake
1 tablespoon
  toasted sesame oil

1 tablespoon
  oyster sauce
freshly ground pepper
1 onion, very finely
  chopped
2 cm (¾ in) ginger,
  very finely chopped
1 garlic clove,
  very finely chopped

Sauce
6 tablespoons
  soy sauce
6 tablespoons
  rice vinegar
1 teaspoon sugar
1 tablespoon
  sesame oil

For the filling, roughly chop the Chinese cabbage, place in a bowl and sprinkle with the salt. Leave for 10 minutes, then squeeze out the excess liquid with your hands. If you are using white cabbage, cook it in boiling water for 2 minutes, then roughly chop and squeeze out the excess liquid with your hands. Place the pork, soy sauce, sake, sesame oil, oyster sauce and pepper in a large bowl. Knead together for 3 minutes, then add the rest of the filling ingredients. Mix together well.

To make the gyoza, place 1 teaspoon of filling in the middle of each gyoza wrapper. Moisten around the edge with a wet finger. Fold in half, holding the bottom of the gyoza with the thumb and the left middle finger and pinching one end. Close to the pinched end, make an S shape using both index fingers. Pinch the S closed to form a pleat and repeat until you reach the other end of the gyoza. Place on a plate and press lightly so the base of the gyoza is nice and flat. If you want to make things easier for yourself, simply fold and seal the edges. The gyoza will still taste the same!

Combine all the sauce ingredients and set aside in the refrigerator. To cook the gyoza, heat some sunflower oil and sesame oil (about 1 tablespoon of each) in a frying pan, tilting the pan so the oil covers the whole base of the pan. Place the gyoza in the pan and cook on medium heat. Once the bases of the gyoza are golden brown, pour in the water and cover the pan. Cook for about 7 minutes, still on medium heat. Remove the lid and let the rest of the water evaporate. Place a large plate on the frying pan and carefully turn over the plate and the frying pan together, so the browned sides of the gyoza are facing upward. Serve with the sauce while the gyoza are still hot.

GYOZA

餃子パーティー

01

02

03

04

GYOZA (CONTINUED)

DEEP-FRIED LAMB AND CILANTRO GYOZA
羊と香菜の揚げ餃子

SERVES 6 (4–5 GYOZA PER PERSON)
30 MINS PREPARATION TIME
10 MINS COOKING TIME

1 package (25–30) gyoza
   wrappers

oil, for deep-frying

Filling
300 g (10½ oz) ground
   lamb
1 red onion,
   roughly chopped
½ bunch cilantro,
   chopped
1 garlic clove,
   finely chopped
2 cm (¾ in) ginger,
   finely chopped
2 teaspoons soy sauce
1 teaspoon fish sauce
1 pinch raw
   (demerara) sugar
1 tablespoon
   toasted sesame oil

Sauce
100 g (3½ oz) cherry
   tomatoes, chopped
1 shallot,
   finely chopped
½ bunch cilantro,
   chopped
juice of ½ organic lime
4 tablespoons
   fish sauce
2 tablespoons olive oil
½ head garlic,
   finely chopped
½ teaspoon chili powder

Combine all the filling ingredients, kneading them together well for at least 3 minutes. Make the gyoza in the same way as the pork gyoza (see p. 194). Mix together all the sauce ingredients in a bowl and set aside in the refrigerator. Pour a 4 cm (1½ in) depth of oil into a saucepan and heat to 170°C (325°F). Add the gyoza and cook for 8 minutes, turning occasionally. Drain on paper towels. Serve the gyoza with the sauce while they are still hot.

TOFU, FENNEL AND PRAWN GYOZA
海老と豆腐の蒸し餃子

SERVES 6 (4–5 GYOZA PER PERSON)
30 MINS PREPARATION TIME + **30 MINS** RESTING TIME
10 MINS COOKING TIME

1 package (25–30) gyoza
   wrappers

Filling
100 g (3½ oz) tofu
200g (7 oz) large raw
   prawns (shrimp)
½ fennel bulb, chopped
   + 1 teaspoon salt
1 spring onion
   (scallion), chopped
1 tablespoon potato
   starch
1 tablespoon oyster sauce
1 pinch salt
1 tablespoon toasted
   sesame oil
freshly ground pepper

Sauce
5 tablespoons
   soy sauce
5 tablespoons
   black vinegar
1 tablespoon
   toasted sesame oil
3 cm (1¼ in) ginger,
   cut into very
   thin matchsticks

For the filling, wrap the tofu in paper towels and place on a plate. Place a board on top of the tofu and a bowl of water on top of the board as a weight. Let the tofu drain for 30 minutes. Peel the prawns, then chop them with a large knife until they have a paste-like texture. Chop the fennel and toss with the salt, then leave for 10 minutes before squeezing out the excess liquid with your hands. Unwrap the drained tofu and use your hands to mash it well in a bowl. Add all the filling ingredients. Make the gyoza in the same way as the pork gyoza (see p. 194). Mix together all the sauce ingredients in a bowl and set aside in the refrigerator. Heat a steamer or bring a saucepan of water to a boil and place a bamboo steamer basket on top. To prevent the gyoza from sticking, line the steamer with parchment paper. Place the gyoza in the steamer, without letting them touch each other, and cook for about 8 minutes on medium heat. Take the basket to the table and enjoy the gyoza straight out of it, dipping them in the sauce before eating.

SHOGAYAKI
STIR-FRIED PORK WITH GINGER SAUCE

生姜焼き

SERVES 4
5 MINS PREPARATION TIME + **15 MINS** MARINATING TIME
15 MINS COOKING TIME

Marinade
2 tablespoons sake
1 tablespoon sugar
1 tablespoon mirin
2½ tablespoons soy sauce
3 cm (1¼ in) ginger, grated

600 g (1 lb 5 oz) pork belly, cut into 5–6 mm (¼ in) thick slices
¼ white cabbage
1 organic lemon, cut into quarters
vegetable oil, for frying

Combine the marinade ingredients in a bowl. Add the pork and leave to marinate for 15 minutes. Slice the cabbage very thinly using a mandoline, then divide evenly between four large serving plates and place a lemon quarter alongside. Heat the oil in a frying pan on high heat and add the drained pork. Sauté for 2 to 3 minutes, turning the meat to brown on both sides. Be careful, as the pork can easily burn—if the temperature is too hot, reduce the heat to medium. Add the marinade and cook the pork in the marinade until it is slightly caramelized and coats the pork. Arrange the pork alongside the cabbage. Drizzle the pork and cabbage with marinade. Squeeze the lemon over the top, if you like, then serve immediately.

OMURAISU
STUFFED OMELETTE
オムライス

SERVES 4
20 MINS PREPARATION TIME
15 MINS COOKING TIME (PER PERSON)

100 g (3½ oz) boneless
  chicken thigh
1 tablespoon vegetable oil
1 small pat of butter
½ onion, roughly chopped
4 mushrooms, thinly sliced
4 bowls of cooked rice
  (see p. 10)

4 tablespoons tomato
  sauce (ketchup) +
  extra to serve
salt and pepper

Omelette
8 eggs
salt
butter

Cut the chicken into 2 cm (¾ in) cubes. Heat the oil and butter in a frying pan on medium heat, then add the chicken and onion. Sauté until they are cooked, then add the mushrooms and rice. If the rice grains have stuck together, sauté until they are separated and heated through. Add the tomato sauce, stirring to coat all the grains of rice. Season with salt and pepper if needed, then set aside in a bowl.

Make 4 individual omelettes. Beat together 2 eggs per omelette with a pinch of salt. Heat a frying pan on a medium heat and add a small pat of butter. Pour in the beaten eggs and spread them quickly over the base of the pan to make a thin, flat omelette. Lower the heat, place a quarter of the tomato rice in the middle of the omelette and wrap the omelette around the rice. Repeat for each serving.

Place the omelettes on plates and serve with tomato sauce on top.

AGEBITASHI
FRIED VEGETABLES MARINATED IN DASHI
揚げ浸し

SERVES 4

20 MINS PREPARATION TIME
15 MINS COOKING TIME
2 HRS MARINATING TIME

Marinade
200 ml (7 fl oz) dashi
    (see p. 12)
90 ml (3 fl oz) soy sauce
2½ tablespoons mirin
2½ tablespoons rice vinegar

1 eggplant
2 asparagus spears
1 red pepper
¼ small squash
3 cm (1¼ in) lotus root
sunflower oil, for deep-frying

Combine all the marinade ingredients in a bowl large enough to hold the vegetables later. Roughly chop the eggplant into 3 cm (1¼ in) chunks, then soak in salted water for 5 minutes. Eggplant is like a sponge, so to prevent it from absorbing too much oil, it is better to do this before cooking it (and it will keep its pretty purple color that way). Dry the eggplant well, otherwise the oil will splatter. Cut each asparagus spears into 3 pieces. Remove the seeds, stem and white membrane from the pepper. Cut in half lengthwise, then cut into 2 cm (¾ in) pieces. Peel the squash unevenly, leaving some skin on for color, and cut into 1 cm (½ in) slices. Peel the lotus root and cut into 1 cm (½ in) slices.

Pour a 4 cm (1½ in) depth of oil into a saucepan, then heat on medium heat until it reaches 170°C (325°F). Cook the eggplant until it is lightly browned and tender, then drain well on paper towels. Add to the marinade. Add some more oil to the pan and fry the pepper, asparagus, squash and lotus root until they are cooked and their colors are bright (I like them to stay a little crisp so I can fully savor them). Be careful not to fry too many vegetables at the same time as it lowers the temperature of the oil. Drain in the same way as the eggplant and add to the marinade. Let the vegetables marinate for at least 2 hours—they are even better the next day.

TAI ZUKE DON
SEA BREAM
ON RICE
鯛の漬け丼

SERVES 4

25 MINS PREPARATION TIME

Marinade
½ brown onion
4 tablespoons soy sauce
2 tablespoons mirin
2 teaspoons toasted sesame seeds

400 g (14 oz) sea bream fillet
4 bowls of cooked rice (see p. 10)
1 extra-fresh egg yolk
1 chive, finely chopped

For the marinade, peel and slice the onion very thinly in the direction of the grain. Combine it with the soy sauce, mirin and sesame seeds. Slice the bream thinly and combine with the marinade, then let it marinate for 15 minutes. Serve the rice in large bowls and arrange the bream and onions from the marinade on top. Spoon a tablespoon of the marinade over the rice. Place the egg yolk in the middle and sprinkle with chives.

SABA NO MISONI

MACKEREL SIMMERED IN MISO

鯖の味噌煮

SERVES 4

25 MINS PREPARATION TIME

15 MINS COOKING TIME

8 mackerel fillets—or 4, if they are large
350 ml (12 fl oz) water
150 ml (5 fl oz) sake
2½ tablespoons mirin
2 tablespoons soy sauce
2½ tablespoons sugar
3 tablespoons miso

Garnish—optional
leek and ginger, cut into very thin matchsticks

Place the mackerel fillets in a large frying pan in a single layer. Add all the other ingredients except the miso and bring to the boil. Reduce the heat to medium and cook for 6 minutes, spooning the sauce over the mackerel from time to time and skimming as needed. Scoop 4 spoonfuls of the sauce into a bowl and blend in the miso, stirring to dissolve, then pour back into the pan. Reduce the sauce, continuing to cook on low heat for about 10 minutes—watch it, to make sure the sauce doesn't burn! Serve on individual plates, drizzled with the sauce. If you like, garnish with leek and ginger.

TONKATSU
BREADED PORK
とんかつ

SERVES 4
8 MINS PREPARATION TIME
12 MINS COOKING TIME

4 rounded tablespoons all-purpose flour
2 eggs, beaten
50 g (1¾ oz) panko breadcrumbs
4 slices pork neck (collar)*, about 2 cm (¾ in) thick
  vegetable oil, for frying
tonkatsu sauce**

Place the flour, beaten eggs and panko in separate shallow
bowls. Dip the pork first in the flour, then in the egg, then in
the panko (press the panko onto the meat with your hands, so
it sticks well). Gently remove any excess panko from the pork.
Take a frying pan that is large enough to fit all the pieces of
pork in a single layer (or cook it in two batches). Pour in a 2 cm
(¾ in) depth of oil and heat to 170°C (325°F). Add the pork and
cook for about 3 minutes on each side until nice and golden
brown. Take out the pork and drain on paper towels, then cut into
2 cm (¾ in) strips. Drizzle with tonkatsu sauce to serve.

* This is a cut with an ideal amount of fat, which the Japanese
enjoy, but pork loin can be used instead.

** Tonkatsu sauce is made from fruit and spices. If you can't find
it in an Asian grocery store, you can make it yourself by mixing
together 3 tablespoons Worcestershire sauce, 3 tablespoons
tomato sauce, 1 tablespoon oyster sauce, 1 teaspoon sugar and
1 teaspoon lemon juice.

TORI DANGO NABE

CHICKEN MEATBALL HOTPOT

鶏団子鍋

❋ NIRA
韮 にら
garlic
chives
mild garlic
aroma

SERVES 4
20 MINS PREPARATION TIME
15 MINS COOKING TIME

½–1 lettuce, such as
 red oak or iceberg
1 leek (white part)
1 bunch nira*
10 fresh shiitake
 mushrooms
1 package of tofu
 (about 400 g/14 oz)
1 bunch sorrel
2 handfuls arugula

Chicken meatballs
350 g (12 oz) ground
 chicken
1 egg
2 tablespoons
 potato starch
½ onion, very
 finely chopped
2 cm (¾ in) ginger,
 finely chopped
4 scallops, finely
 chopped—optional
1 teaspoon soy sauce
freshly ground pepper

Soup
1.2 liters (42 fl oz)
 dashi (see p. 12)
4 cm x 4 cm (1½ in
 x 1½ in) piece kombu
100 ml (3½ fl oz) sake
2 tablespoons mirin
2 tablespoons soy sauce
1 pinch salt

Sauce
4 tablespoons soy sauce
2 tablespoons rice vinegar
juice of ¼ yuzu

Condiments
thinly sliced spring
 onions (scallions)
shichimi (Japanese
 7-spice mix)
yuzu koshou (savory
 yuzu and chili jam)

Wash the lettuce and separate the leaves. Cut the leek into 2 cm (¾ in) slices on the diagonal. Cut the nira in half. Remove the stems from the shiitake mushrooms. Cut the tofu into 3 cm (1¼ in) cubes. Place the sorrel and arugula on a plate.

Combine all the chicken meatball ingredients well in a bowl, then set aside in the refrigerator.

Place all the soup ingredients in a pot with a lid and heat on medium heat. When it comes to a boil, remove the kombu. Add half the tofu, leeks and shiitake. Add a third of the chicken, shaping it into balls using two spoons. Cover the pot and cook the meatballs for about 5 minutes. Once they are cooked, they will rise to the surface.

Take the pot directly to the table on a burner. Add the lettuce leaves and let guests help themselves to the soup, transferring it to their bowls. The soup is already well seasoned, but if you want you can add 1 or 2 teaspoons of sauce to your bowl. Add condiments to your taste. Gradually add the different foods to the pot and repeat the cooking process as you go, depending on the appetites of your guests.

ZOSUI
LEFTOVER NABE RICE SOUP
雑炊

SERVES 4
3 MINS PREPARATION TIME
8 MINS COOKING TIME

leftover nabe (see p. 212)
4 bowls of cooked rice (see p. 10)
2 eggs
5 spring onions (scallions), thinly sliced

Take out any leftover nabe ingredients (if there are any!) from the soup. Separate the grains of rice well with a spatula, or rinse it briefly, before adding it to the leftover nabe. Cover and cook for about 5 minutes on a medium heat. Remove the lid. Beat the eggs in a bowl and pour them in, cover again (without mixing in the eggs) and turn off the heat. Wait 3 minutes for the eggs to cook. Sprinkle with the spring onions. Serve in individual bowls.

Note: The rice soup is the best part of the nabe, as the broth will have absorbed all the flavors of the ingredients. Even if you're quite full, it is hard to resist!

TONYU NABE
SOY MILK HOTPOT
豆乳鍋

SERVES 4
20 MINS PREPARATION TIME
20 MINS COOKING TIME

1 leek (white part)
1 bunch nira*
½ Chinese cabbage
10 fresh shiitake
  mushrooms
1 carrot
½ white radish (daikon)
300 g (10½ oz) sliced pork
1 package tofu
  (about 400 g/14 oz)

600 ml (21 fl oz)
  dashi (see p. 12)
4 cm (1½ in) piece kombu
4 tablespoons brown miso
600 ml (21 fl oz) soy milk
2 tablespoons mirin
2 teaspoons soy sauce
1 pinch salt

Condiment
shichimi*

Cut the leek on the diagonal into 2 cm (¾ in) pieces. Cut the nira into 4 cm (1½ in) lengths. Cut the Chinese cabbage into 3 pieces. Remove the stems from the shiitakes. Peel the carrot and cut into lengths on the diagonal, then cut each piece in half. Peel the radish and slice into 5 mm (¼ in) rounds, then cut each round in half. Cut the pork into 3 cm (1¼ in) pieces. Cut the tofu into 4 cm (1½ in) cubes.

Put the dashi and kombu in a pot with a lid. Turn on the heat and add half of the leek, Chinese cabbage, carrot and radish. Cover and bring to a boil, then cook on medium heat for 10 minutes. In a small bowl, blend the miso into a small amount of the soy milk, then add to the pot, along with the rest of the soy milk, the mirin, soy sauce and some salt, if necessary. Add the pork, shiitakes and tofu (however much you want). Cover and continue to cook on low or medium heat for about 10 minutes, making sure the soy milk doesn't come to a boil.

* NIRA
菲 にら
garlic
chives
mild garlic
aroma

* SHICHIMI
= 七味
Japanese spice mix
with 7 ingredients

(mandarin zest,
sesame seeds, sansho
pepper, red chili...)

Bring the pot to the table on a burner (if you have something more powerful such as an electric plate or portable gas ring, even better). The hotpot should be simmering, so it can cook new added foods. Add the nira at the last moment, because it cooks very quickly. Let guests serve themselves from the hotpot and sprinkle their bowls with shichimi to their taste. Once the precooked food has all been eaten, add the remaining ingredients as you go, so they are cooked perfectly.

Note: You can make a "Oiya risotto" from this dish by adding some precooked rice. Precooked udon noodles added to the broth are also very good.

SUKIYAKI
BEEF HOTPOT
すき焼き

SERVES 4
15 MINS PREPARATION TIME
15 MINS COOKING TIME

* SHUNGIKU
= 春菊
Edible chrysanthemum

Widely eaten in Japan, especially in winter

* SHIRATAKI
= 白滝
White vermicelli made from konnyaku
You can find it in Japanese supermarkets

1 package shirataki*
  (about 400 g/14 oz)
1 pack shimeji mushrooms
1 leek (white part)
½ bunch shungiku*
  or arugula
¼ Chinese cabbage
500 g (1 lb 2 oz) tofu
600 g (1 lb 5 oz) sliced beef
4 extra-fresh organic eggs
100–200 ml (3½–7 fl oz)
  dashi (see p. 12)
2 packages precooked
  udon noodles

Sukiyaki broth
100 ml (3½ fl oz) soy sauce
100 ml (3½ fl oz) sake
3 tablespoons raw sugar

Rinse the shirataki well and drain. Cut into 3 lengths. Wash the shimeji and roughly separate them. Cut the leek into 2 cm (¾ in) slices on the diagonal. Wash the shungiku, then cut across into 2 sections. Wash the Chinese cabbage and cut into 3 pieces. Cut the tofu into 3 cm (1¼ in) cubes.

Place half of the prepared ingredients in a pot, ideally side by side. (If necessary, use a frying pan that doesn't leave too much space around the ingredients.) Mix together the sukiyaki broth ingredients and pour over, then cover and cook on medium heat for about 10 minutes. Add half of the beef.

Once the vegetables are cooked, bring the pot to the table on a burner. Break the eggs into individual bowls and lightly beat with chopsticks. Let guests serve themselves, dipping the different foods in the beaten egg in their bowl. Gradually add more foods to the pot as they run out and repeat the cooking process as you go, according to the appetites of your guests. If there is not enough liquid, add some dashi. Right at the end of cooking (when there are no more ingredients in the sauce), add the cooked udon noodles.

道具屋 **KITCHENWARE**

For those in search of kitchen tools or utensils, there are still some specialized neighborhoods in Tokyo, such as Kappa-bashi street, that are dedicated to kitchenware. Japanese utensils are very varied. There are special knives for small fish, big fish, long fish, vegetables... bowls for crushing sesame seeds, different graters for wasabi, ginger and daikon.

Of course, you could make do with just one knife, but when you love to cook (and cook well), these different tools are seen as essential, even compulsory.

KOROKKE
POTATO CROQUETTES
コロッケ

SERVES 4 (MAKES 8 CROQUETTES)
30 MINS PREPARATION TIME
45 MINS COOKING TIME

1 onion
sunflower oil, for frying
150 g (5½ oz) ground
  pork
1 teaspoon soy sauce
1 tablespoon mirin
600 g (1 lb 5 oz) potatoes
  of your choice
  (I use bintje)

2 pinches natural salt
freshly ground pepper
110 g (3¾ oz/¾ cup)
  all-purpose flour
2 eggs, beaten
90 g (3¼ oz/1½ cups) panko
  breadcrumbs
tonkatsu sauce

Chop the onion. Heat 1 tablespoon of oil in a frying pan on medium heat and sauté the onion until translucent. Add the pork and sauté for about 4 minutes, or until the pork is cooked through. Season with the soy sauce and mirin. Cook the potatoes in their skins, ideally whole, in a large saucepan of boiling water. (If you are short on time, cut them in half.) Drain and peel. Mash the potatoes roughly in a bowl with a fork or spatula, without turning them into a purée. Add the pork and onion mixture and season with salt and pepper. Shape into 8 croquettes.

Take 3 shallow bowls: put the flour in the first one, beaten eggs in the second, and panko in the third. Dip the patties in the flour, then in the egg and finally in the panko. Pour a 3 cm (1¼ in) depth of oil into a pan and heat to 180°C (350°F). Fry the croquettes until nicely browned. Drain on paper towels and serve immediately, with or without the tonkatsu sauce.

HIYASI CHUKA
NOODLES WITH CHICKEN AND CUCUMBER
冷やし中華

SERVES 4

25 MINS PREPARATION TIME
25 MINS COOKING TIME

✳ TOBANJAN

= 豆板醤
Chinese fermented bean and chili paste. You can replace it with 1 teaspoon brown miso and ½ teaspoon mild chili flakes.

1 boneless chicken thigh
2 x 3 mm (⅛ in)
   slices of ginger, unpeeled
2 eggs
pinch of sugar
toasted sesame oil
1 cucumber

4 packages of dried
   ramen noodles

Sauce
½ leek (white part)
3 cm (1¼ in) ginger
4 tablespoons soy sauce
2 tablespoons rice vinegar
2 tablespoons tahini,**
   for a creamier
   sauce—optional

1 teaspoon tobanjan*
2 tablespoons chicken
   stock (use the liquid
   from cooking the chicken)
1½ tablespoons sugar
2 tablespoons
   toasted sesame oil

Bring a saucepan of water to a boil, then add the chicken and slices of ginger. Reduce the heat to low and cook for about 15 minutes. Remove from the heat and let the chicken cool in the cooking liquid. Beat the eggs with a pinch of sugar, then fry in a frying pan with a little sesame oil to make a thin omelette. Cut the omelette into 3 pieces, place the pieces on top of one another and cut into very thin strips. Slice the cucumber on the diagonal, then cut into matchsticks. Cut the chicken into 1 cm (½ in) strips. For the sauce, chop the leek and ginger very finely, then combine with the other sauce ingredients in a bowl.

Cook the noodles for the length of time indicated on the package. Drain and rinse well under cold running water to remove any excess starch—this is very important for getting the right texture. Place the chicken, omelette and cucumber on the noodles and pour over the sauce just before serving.

** You can buy tahini (sesame paste) in Middle Eastern or organic food stores, and in Japanese supermarkets under the name neri goma.

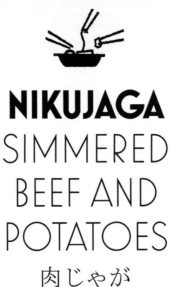

NIKUJAGA
SIMMERED BEEF AND POTATOES
肉じゃが

SERVES 4
15 MINS PREPARATION TIME
30 MINS COOKING TIME

1 brown onion
5 large potatoes
  or 10 small ones
2 tablespoons first
  cold-pressed sesame oil
200 g (7 oz) sliced beef
360 ml (12½ fl oz) dashi
  (see p. 12)

2½ tablespoons soy sauce
2½ tablespoons mirin
2½ tablespoons sake
2 tablespoons
  raw (demerara) sugar
1 tablespoon toasted
  sesame seeds

Cut the onion into 2 cm (¾ in) slices on the diagonal. Peel the potatoes and cut them into quarters (or in half for small potatoes). Heat the sesame oil in a pan. Add the meat slice by slice, so the slices don't stick together, and sauté for 1 minute. Add the potatoes and onion and sauté for another minute. Add the dashi and season with the soy sauce, mirin, sake and sugar. Bring to a boil, then reduce the heat to medium, cover the pan and simmer for 10 minutes. Remove the lid and simmer for another 15 minutes to reduce the liquid, stirring from time to time. Remove from the heat when the liquid has reduced by one-third. Serve in bowls and sprinkle with sesame seeds.

NANBANZUKE
HORSE MACKEREL
ESCABECHE
南蛮漬け

SERVES 4
15 MINS PREPARATION TIME
10 MINS COOKING TIME
15 MINS MARINATING TIME

Marinade
125 ml (4 fl oz/½ cup) soy sauce
125 ml (4 fl oz/½ cup) rice vinegar
2½ tablespoons water
1 tablespoon raw (demerara) sugar
3 cm x 3 cm (1¼ in x 1¼ in) piece kombu seaweed
chopped red chili—optional

½ red onion, sliced
1 carrot, cut into thin matchsticks
2 cm (¾ in) ginger, cut into thin matchsticks
12 small horse mackerel or other mackerel
flour, for dusting
sunflower oil, for frying

Combine all the marinade ingredients in a bowl, adding a little chopped chili, if you like. Add the onion, carrot and ginger to the marinade. Remove the heads of the horse mackerel and gut them—or ask your fishmonger to do this for you. Dry them well inside with paper towels. Put some flour on a plate and dust the mackerel with flour, shaking gently to remove any excess. Pour a 3 cm (1¼ in) depth of oil into a pan and heat to about 160°C (315°F). Fry the mackerel for about 10 minutes, turning several times, until they are crunchy and a nice golden color all over. Drain on paper towels, then add directly to the marinade and mix gently. Leave to marinate for at least 15 minutes. (This is very good even the next day.)

SHIOBUTA WITH SPICY MISO SAUCE

SALTED PORK WITH SPICY MISO SAUCE

茹で塩豚の辛み味噌

SERVES 4–6

20 MINS PREPARATION TIME + **1–4 DAYS** MARINATING TIME

1 HR 10 MINS COOKING TIME

✳ GOCHUJANG

= 고추장

Korean fermented soy bean and chili paste. Slightly sweet and very spicy, this Korean condiment is popular in Japan.

500 g (1 lb 2 oz) pork belly, bones removed
15 g (½ oz) coarse sea salt

3 cm x 3 cm (1¼ in x 1¼ in) piece kombu seaweed

Sauce
2 tablespoons miso
1 tablespoon gochujang*
1 tablespoon raw (demerara) sugar
1 tablespoon mirin
2 tablespoons toasted sesame oil
1 teaspoon soy sauce
1 tablespoon sesame seeds
1 teaspoon chopped ginger
½ garlic clove, grated
3 cm (1¼ in) leek (white part), chopped

To serve
3 cm (1¼ in) leek (white part)
½ lettuce, leaves separated
8 shiso (perilla) leaves
your choice of herbs

A few days ahead of time, rub the pork with the salt and wrap in plastic wrap. Marinate the pork in the refrigerator for at least 1 to 2 days, or up to 4 days.

Place the pork in a saucepan. Cover with water and add the kombu. Place on medium heat, and once the water comes to the boil, cook the pork on low heat for 1 hour. Turn off the heat and let the pork cool in the cooking liquid. When it is lukewarm, remove the pork and cut into 1 cm (½ in) thick slices. Cut the leek into very thin matchsticks. Place the slices of pork on a large plate with the lettuce, shiso, leek and herbs. Combine all the sauce ingredients in a small bowl. To serve, place the pork on a lettuce leaf, add a teaspoonful of sauce and some herbs, then roll up the lettuce leaf around the pork, sauce and herbs.

Note: Open your mouth wide to eat these! I also like to add a little Japanese rice to the lettuce roll. This dish from Korea is now very popular with the Japanese. My mother made the same dish, but instead of pork she used sardine sashimi. That version is also delicious if you can find very fresh sardines at the market.

NIBUTA CHASHU
PORK SIMMERED WITH STAR ANISE
煮豚

SERVES 4–6

15 MINS PREPARATION TIME

1 HR 15 MINS COOKING TIME

1 leek
3 cm (1¼ in) piece ginger,
   unpeeled
500 g (1 lb 2 oz) pork—
   choose a well-marbled
   cut, such as neck (collar)
3 star anise
200 ml (7 fl oz) sake
200 ml (7 fl oz) soy sauce
70 g (2½ oz) raw
   (demerara) sugar

2 tablespoons
   oyster sauce
about 1 liter
   (35 fl oz/4 cups) water
4 boiled eggs, cooked
   to your preference—
   I like soft-boiled

Garnish
5 cm (2 in) leek (white
   part), finely shredded

Cut the leek into 3 sections, slice the ginger into 3 pieces and cut the pork into 2 or 3 pieces. Place all the ingredients except the eggs in a saucepan, ideally one that will hold the pieces of pork in a single layer. Bring to a boil, then reduce the heat to low. Cook the pork for about 30 minutes with the lid on, and then for another 30 minutes uncovered. Take out the pork, but return the cooking liquid to high heat and let it simmer until it is reduced by half. Return the pieces of pork to the pan, turning to coat with the sauce. At the same time, add the boiled eggs, leaving them whole. Turn off the heat and let the dish rest a little. Slice the pork. Dress with sauce and garnish with shredded leek. The meat can also be served on ramen (see p. 46).

Note: You can keep the sauce in a small jar for 2 weeks and use it to make ramen soup (see p. 46), or as a seasoning instead of soy sauce (for stir-frying meat, for example).

ROLL KYABETSU
JAPANESE STUFFED CABBAGE
ロールキャベツ

SERVES 4

20 MINS PREPARATION TIME

45 MINS COOKING TIME

8 leaves Savoy
   cabbage
karashi (Japanese mustard)
chopped spring
   onion (scallion)

1 onion, finely chopped
2 cm (¾ in) ginger,
   finely chopped
1 tablespoon soy sauce
1 pinch salt

Stuffing
2 dried shiitake mushrooms
300 ml (10½ fl oz) water
500 g (1 lb 2 oz) ground
   pork
50 g (1¾ oz) cooked rice
   (see p. 10)

Broth
1 tablespoon soy sauce
2 tablespoons mirin
1 teaspoon salt
2 tablespoons sake
400 ml (14 fl oz) dashi
   (see p. 12)

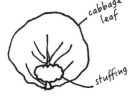

cabbage leaf

stuffing

For the stuffing, soak the dried shiitakes in the water for at least 3 hours, until they are soft (you can do this the day before). Drain, reserving the soaking liquid for the broth. Remove the stems from the shiitakes and finely dice the caps. Combine with the rest of the stuffing ingredients, kneading everything together well.

Bring a large saucepan of water to a boil and blanch each cabbage leaf in the water for about 1 minute. This softens the leaves so they can be wrapped around the stuffing. Place an eighth of the stuffing on a cabbage leaf. Fold in the sides and then roll up the leaf to enclose the stuffing. Place the rolls in a saucepan that will hold them in a single, snug layer. Add the broth ingredients and the soaking water from the mushrooms, then bring to a boil on medium heat. Reduce the heat to low, cover with a lid and cook for about 30 minutes until the rolls are tender. Spoon some broth over the rolls from time to time, if necessary. Serve with Japanese mustard and chopped spring onion.

SUSHI NIGHT

寿司パーティー

SERVES 4–6
40 MINS PREPARATION TIME
40 MINS COOKING TIME

FILLINGS

1 cucumber
4 eggs
1 tablespoon raw (demerara) sugar
1 tablespoon soy sauce
150 g (5½ oz) sashimi-grade organic salmon fillet
150 g (5½ oz) sashimi-grade tuna fillet
10 large raw prawns (shrimp)
5 okra pods
10 shiso (perilla) leaves
10 lettuce leaves—oak leaf,
  or whatever you prefer
1 jar ikura (salted salmon roe)

10 sheets nori seaweed, each cut into 4 squares

Cut the cucumber into thin batons about 4 cm (1½ in) long. Make a Japanese omelette (see p. 20) with the eggs, sugar and soy sauce, then cut into 4 cm (1½ in) slices. Cut the salmon fillet into two 5 cm (2 in) wide pieces, then into 6 mm (¼ in) slices. Cut the tuna into 6 mm (¼ in) slices. Remove the heads of the prawns and insert skewers along their backs. Cook them in boiling water for 4 minutes, then remove the skewers. Peel the prawns and carefully split open their belly without cutting them in half. Cook the okra in salted water for 1 minute, then drain and cut in half lengthwise. Wash the shiso and lettuce leaves. Arrange all the ingredients on a serving platter, and let people assemble their choice of sushi at the table.

01

02

03

SUSHIZU すし酢

SUSHI VINEGAR

300 ml (10½ fl oz) rice vinegar
6 tablespoons white sugar
6 teaspoons salt
3 cm (1¼ in) piece of kombu seaweed, diced

Heat all the ingredients in a saucepan on low heat, stirring to dissolve the sugar and salt. Just before it comes to a boil, remove from the heat and keep in a container (with the kombu left in) in the refrigerator.

SUMESHI 酢飯

VINEGARED SUSHI RICE

600 g (1 lb 5 oz) uncooked rice
135 ml (4½ fl oz) sushi vinegar—about 10%
  of the weight of the cooked rice

Cook the rice in the normal way (see p. 10), reducing the amount of water used by 4 tablespoons. Place the cooked rice in a large bowl while it is still hot. Pour in the vinegar over a spatula (let the vinegar run down the spatula, so it is sprinkled over the whole surface of the rice). Mix the rice by "cutting" it on an angle with the spatula, cooling the rice with a fan at the same time. Be careful not to crush the grains of rice. Cover with a damp tea towel and set aside. Never put the rice in the refrigerator, as this completely changes its texture.

Note: The sushi vinegar will keep for 3 weeks in the refrigerator, so it's worth making extra for the next time you want sushi.

巻き寿司 MAKI TEMAKI

TEMAKI

To make temaki, cut a nori sheet into 4 squares. Lay a square piece in the palm of your hand and place some rice on the nori along the diagonal. Arrange your choice of filling in the same direction and roll it up on the diagonal as well. If you want to add more than one filling, use a sheet of nori cut into 2 rectangles. Follow the same method but place the rice on one side only, then you have a longer piece of nori that can be rolled around more fillings to make a cone.

01

03

02

01

03

MAKI

To make maki, place a sheet of nori (or half a sheet for thinner maki) on a sushi mat. With wet hands, take a small handful of rice and spread it along the nori. Do not use too much rice or it will spill out when you roll it up. You need to leave 1 cm (½ in) nori uncovered along the lower edge (the one you start rolling from) and 3 cm (1¼ in) on the top edge (farthest away from you). Add your choice of fillings, for example: salmon + avocado + omelette + cucumber. Try to stack them so you don't have more than two or three horizontal lines of filling. Using the mat, lift the edge of the nori that is closest to you, pressing lightly on the fillings to keep them in place. Gently roll until the edges of the nori meet up. Place the maki in the middle of the mat (with the join side facing down, so it doesn't come undone) and using the mat, apply slight pressure to form a well-shaped roll. You can also make thinner maki by cutting the nori into 2 rectangles and using one, or at most two, fillings. Use the same method as for the large maki.

02

04

05

SEA BREAM
SASHIMI SALAD
鯛の刺身サラダ

SERVES 4
20 MINS PREPARATION TIME
1 MIN COOKING TIME

½ onion
3 cm (1¼ in) leek
  (white part)
½ turnip
¼ carrot
½ cucumber
½ white radish (daikon)
2 sashimi-grade
  sea bream fillets
your choice of herbs—
  mint, dill, cilantro, etc.

1 tablespoon peanuts,
  toasted and roughly
  chopped

Dressing
2 tablespoons peanut oil
  (or sunflower oil)
1 tablespoon sesame oil
3 tablespoons soy sauce
juice of 1 organic lime
freshly ground pepper

Thinly slice the onion. Discard the outer layer from the leek, then cut the leek into matchsticks, as thin as possible. Soak in water for 10 minutes to soften the flavor, then drain well. Cut the turnip into very thin half-circles, and the rest of the vegetables into matchsticks. Mix all the vegetables together in a bowl. Cut the bream into thin slices, about 6 mm (¼ in) thick. Arrange the vegetables on a large plate, then the bream. Place the leek in the middle, then scatter over the herbs and peanuts.

Just before serving, make the dressing. Combine the two oils and heat in a small saucepan until they start to lightly smoke. Pour the hot oil over the salad, along with the soy sauce, lime juice and pepper. Toss everything together and serve.

Note: Be careful—the oils get very hot; they mustn't ever be left on the heat unattended. Once you can see the mixture smoking, remove from the heat and pour over the salad immediately. This gives a smoky flavor to the dish.

SŌMEN
FRESH NOODLES WITH SAUCE AND TOPPINGS
素麺

SERVES 4
20 MINS PREPARATION TIME
30 MINS COOKING TIME

Mentsuyu sauce
400 ml (14 fl oz) water
150 ml (5 fl oz) mirin
200 ml (7 fl oz) soy sauce
1 teaspoon raw
   (demerara) sugar
1 handful katsuobushi
   (dried bonito flakes)
5 cm (2 in) square
   piece kombu

1 eggplant
1 tablespoon sesame oil

Toppings
3 eggs
1 pinch raw
   (demerara) sugar
½ cucumber
8 okra pods
1 spring onion (scallion)
½ sheet nori
3 cm (1¼ in) piece ginger,
   grated
toasted sesame seeds

400 g (14 oz) sōmen
   noodles

Place all the mentsuyu sauce ingredients in a saucepan on a low heat. Cook for 20 minutes, then remove from the heat. (You can keep the sauce for 2 weeks in a thoroughly clean jar in the refrigerator.) Cut the eggplant into 3 lengthwise, then into 6 mm (¼ in) thick slices. Heat the sesame oil in a saucepan and sauté the eggplant until golden, then add the mentsuyu sauce. Let it simmer for 5 minutes on medium heat. Take off the heat and allow to cool. (This will keep in the refrigerator for up to 3 days.)

For the toppings, scramble the eggs with the sugar. Cut the cucumber into 5 cm (2 in) sections and then into very thin matchsticks. Cook the okra for 1 minute in boiling water, then slice thinly. Slice the spring onion very finely. Shred the nori.

Note: It is important to cook the noodles just before serving, or they won't have the right texture. Bring a large saucepan of water to the boil. Add the noodles and cook according to the instructions on the package. When they are cooked, drain and rinse the noodles, rubbing them together under running water for 1 minute to completely remove the starch. This step is compulsory!

Arrange the noodles in a large "zaru" bamboo basket with a plate underneath. If you don't have a bamboo basket, just arrange the noodles on a plate. And if you have ice cubes, place a few on the noodles to chill them. Place all the toppings in separate dishes (egg, okra, spring onion, shredded nori, grated ginger and sesame seeds). Dilute the mentsuyu sauce to taste (I like to add half the amount of water), then serve in small individual bowls. To eat, put your choice of toppings in your bowl, dip the noodles in and eat.

Note: Play around with different combinations of toppings! Feel free to add more mentsuyu if the sauce is too diluted.

NIBITASHI
DASHI-COOKED VEGETABLES
煮浸し

SERVES 4

5 MINS PREPARATION TIME
5 MINS COOKING TIME

1 bunch (about 250 g/9 oz) mizuna*
2 sheets abura-age (fried sliced tofu)
300 ml (10½ fl oz) dashi (see p. 12)
1 tablespoon mirin
1 teaspoon soy sauce
1 pinch salt

Wash the mizuna well and cut into 5 cm (2 in) sections. Place the abura-age in a colander. Pour some boiling water over it to remove any excess oil. Turn over and repeat on the other side. Drain and cut into 1 cm (½ in) strips. In a medium saucepan, bring the dashi, mirin, soy sauce and salt to a boil. Add the mizuna and abura-age and stir for 1 minute. Divide the mizuna and abura-age among four small bowls, then pour the dashi over the top.

* MIZUNA
= 水菜
A native Japanese
lettuce.
Mild mustard-
leaf flavor.
  Very good for salads.

LOTUS ROOT AND HIJIKI SALAD
ひじきと蓮根のサラダ

SERVES 4
20 MINS PREPARATION TIME
3 MINS COOKING TIME

Dressing
2 tablespoons olive oil
1 tablespoon soy sauce
1 tablespoon rice vinegar
1 pinch coarse natural salt
½ garlic clove, grated

5 g (⅛ oz) dried hijiki* seaweed
¼ red onion
100 g (3½ oz) lotus root
1 pinch salt
20 g (¾ oz) mizuna

* HIJIKI
= ひじき
ME-HIJIKI
(hijiki leaves or buds)

HIJIKI
longer like mini
black noodles

In a small bowl, mix the dressing ingredients together well.

Soak the hijiki in water for 15 minutes, then drain. Slice the onion very thinly, then soak in water for 10 minutes and drain well. Peel the lotus root and cut into thin rounds. If the root is large, cut each round in half. Soak in water for 5 minutes, then drain. Bring a saucepan of water to a boil with the salt. First cook the lotus root for 1 to 2 minutes: it should still be crisp. Drain well. In the same water, cook the hijiki (also for barely a minute) and drain well. Wash the mizuna and cut into 3 cm (1¼ in) lengths. Assemble the salad in a large bowl, pour the dressing over the top and mix together well before serving.

KATSUO NO TATAKI
BONITO SASHIMI
WITH HERBS
鰹のたたき

SERVES 4

15 MINS PREPARATION TIME + **15 MINS** MARINATING TIME

400 g (14 oz) sashimi-grade bonito
15 cm (6 in) white radish (daikon)
1 garlic clove
3 shiso (perilla) leaves
2 myoga*
1 sudachi**
soy sauce

There are two schools of thought on preparing bonito. The first is to lightly sear the raw bonito on all sides over a gas flame or a straw flame (to be more authentic). As soon as the surface of the bonito changes color, it is plunged into iced water, then drained and patted dry. The second school skips this step. My father prefers the second method because he thinks the first method spoils the texture and aroma of the bonito. Personally, I like both methods very much. By searing the surface, you get the aroma of the slightly smoky skin. So, after this step (or not), cut the bonito into 6 mm (¼ in) slices. Peel and grate the radish, then squeeze out some of the liquid. Slice the garlic into fine slivers. Shred the shiso leaves. Slice the myoga into very thin rounds. Juice the sudachi (you can use another citrus fruit: yuzu, lemon, lime or bergamot) and set aside.

Arrange the slices of bonito on a plate. Scatter the garlic, shiso and myoga over the bonito. Sprinkle with the sudachi juice and top with the grated radish. Marinate in the refrigerator for 15 minutes. Enjoy the sashimi dipped in (not too much!) soy sauce.

✳ MYOGA
= 茗荷
Japanese ginger
The floral buds are eaten fresh and add fragrance to dishes.

✳✳ SUDACHI
= すだち
Japanese citrus fruit like YUZU.
Specialty of Tokushima Prefecture.

NIZAKANA
FISH POACHED IN SOY SAUCE AND SAKE
煮魚

SERVES 4

15 MINS PREPARATION TIME

15 MINS COOKING TIME

4 small (or 2 medium) white fish, such as ocean perch
  or small sea bream, gutted and scaled—
  ask your fishmonger to do this
4 tablespoons soy sauce
4 tablespoons mirin
1 tablespoon raw (demerara) sugar
200 ml (7 fl oz) sake
160 ml (5¼ fl oz) water
1 leek (white part), cut into 3 cm (1¼ in) lengths
4 thin slices ginger, plus more for garnish

Clean the fish thoroughly (especially inside the cavity). Dry with paper towels. Score each side of the fish once or twice on the diagonal. Choose a saucepan large enough to hold the fish in a single layer. (If you have a bamboo leaf, place it in the base of the saucepan, so the fish doesn't stick.) Add the soy sauce, mirin, sugar, sake and water to the pan. Bring to a boil and add the fish, leek and ginger. Cover, leaving the lid slightly ajar. Lower the heat and cook for 5 to 6 minutes on low to medium heat. Remove the lid and cook on medium to high heat for 3 to 4 minutes to reduce the sauce. Baste the fish with the sauce from time to time. Once the fish is cooked and the sauce has thickened, remove from the heat. Serve the fish on individual plates with the slices of ginger and the sauce.

JAPANESE-STYLE STEAK
サイコロステーキ

SERVES 4
15 MINS PREPARATION TIME
10 MINS COOKING TIME

Sauce
5 tablespoons soy sauce
2 tablespoons rice vinegar
juice of ½ organic lemon
1 garlic clove, crushed

4 x 150 g (5½ oz) steaks, ideally well marbled
  and about 2 cm (¾ in) thick
salt
2 tablespoons sake
5 cm (2 in) white radish (daikon), grated

Mix the sauce ingredients together. Take the steaks out of the refrigerator at least half an hour before cooking. Lightly season with salt, then cook the steaks in a frying pan according to your preference. Sprinkle the sake over the steak to add aroma. Remove the steaks from the heat and let them rest for 3 minutes. Cut into cubes and serve on a plate with the grated white radish and the sauce. Dip the steak into the sauce and eat with a little white radish.

APPENDIXES

UTENSILS

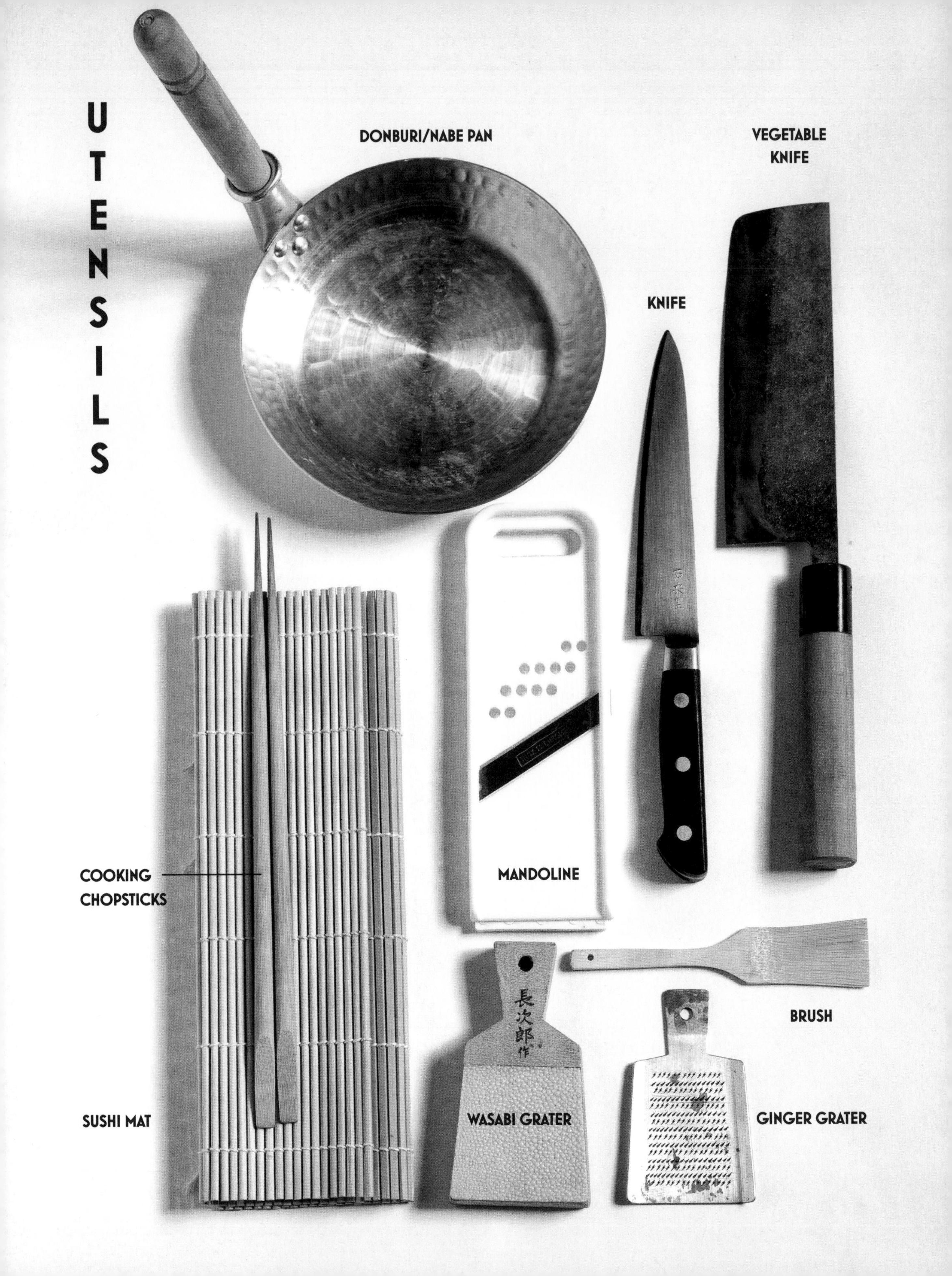
DONBURI/NABE PAN
VEGETABLE KNIFE
KNIFE
COOKING CHOPSTICKS
MANDOLINE
BRUSH
長次郎作
SUSHI MAT
WASABI GRATER
GINGER GRATER

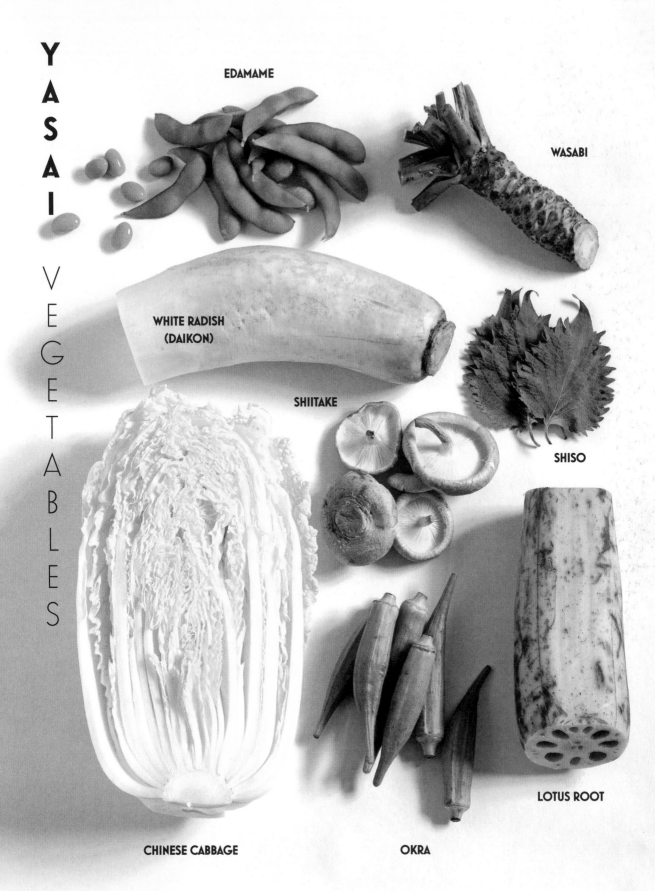

Y A S A I

VEGETABLES

EDAMAME

WASABI

WHITE RADISH
(DAIKON)

SHIITAKE

SHISO

CHINESE CABBAGE

OKRA

LOTUS ROOT

DRIED SHIITAKE

KATSUOBUSHI
(DRIED BONITO FLAKES)

KANBUTSU DRIED INGREDIENTS

WAKAME

SEAWEED SALAD   NORI   HIJIKI

KOMBU

YAMA MOTO YAMA
SINCE 1690

江戸前

E D O M A E

Serving
Suggestion

Roasted Seaweed
Net Weight: 25g (10 Sheets)

Algues Grillees
Poids Net: 25g (10 Feuilles)

Geroestete Algen
Netto: 25g (10 Blätter)

Alghe Tostate
Peso Netto: 25g (10 Fogli)

Alga marina Tostada
Peso Neto: 25g (10 Hojas)

Geroosterd Zeewier
Nettogewicht: 25g (10 Vellen)

Rister Tang
Nettovægh: 25g (10 Plader)

Roasted Tang
Nettovikt: 25g (10 Blad)

M E N

N O O D L E S

COOKED
UDON

MUSHIMEN

RĀMEN

SOBA

SŌMEN

野菜こんぷら

SATSUMA AGE
(FRIED FISHCAKE)

はんぺん

HANPEN
(FISH PASTE)

あぶらあげ
ABURA·AGE

FRITTIERTE TOFU-TASCHE
FRIED SOYBEAN CURD
PATE DE SOJA FRITE
CAGLIATA DI SOIA FRITTA

Netto/Net weight/Poids Net/
Peso Netto : 45G
(3 Stücke/Pieces/Morceaux/Pezzi)

16. 01. 15
L7968

ABURA-AGE
(FRIED TOFU SHEETS)

TOFU

UMEBOSHI
(SALTED PLUM)

徳用
群馬のしらたき

C 193

SHIRATAKI
(KONNYAKU VERMICELLI)

第一家 Spring Home 第一家

TYJ SPRING ROLL PASTRY

春卷皮

SERVING
SUGGESTION
SERVIERVORCHLAG

Manufactured in Singapore by:
第一家食品廠有限公司
Tee Yih Jia Food Manufacturing Pte Ltd
1 Senoko Road Tee Yih Jia Building Singapore 758134
Tel:+65 6880 9888 Fax:+65 6286 2222 Email:tyj@tyjfood.com
Website: www.teeyihjia.com

40

Importé par: Paris Store S.A. 15-21 Rue du Puits-Dixme - SENIA 712, 94657 Thiais Cedex, France
BEST BEFORE DATE / TENMINSTE HOUDBAAR TOT/A CONSOMMER AVANT LE/ MINDESTENS HALTBAR BIS DEN / 此日期前最佳:
DD MM YYYY 日日 月月 年年年年 HH BB TTTT :   24 02 2017

GYOZA
WRAPPERS

SPRING ROLL WRAPPERS

SONO TA OTHER INGREDIENTS

BBQ SAUCE

Use for: marinating meat before barbecuing; dressing raw tofu and strongly flavored salad leaves such as arugula or radicchio. Keeps for: 4 days.

TO MARINATE
400 G (14 OZ) MEAT

4 tablespoons soy sauce
2 tablespoons mirin
1 tablespoon toasted sesame oil
1 garlic clove, grated
⅛ apple, grated
1 teaspoon raw (demerara) sugar
3 cm (1¼ in) leek (white part), chopped
2 teaspoons toasted sesame seeds

Mix all the ingredients together.

CARROT DRESSING

Use for: a fresh, creamy dressing for any salad. Allow 3–4 tablespoons for a salad for 4 people. Keeps for: 4 days.

TO DRESS
SALAD FOR 4 PEOPLE

2½ tablespoons soy sauce
2 tablespoons rice vinegar
2½ tablespoons extra-virgin olive oil
1 tablespoon miso
1 tablespoon tahini or sesame paste
1 tablespoon raw (demerara) sugar
1 garlic clove
1 cm (½ in) ginger, peeled
4 cm (1½ in) carrot, peeled
1 small segment onion, peeled

Purée all the ingredients together using a stick blender.

KOMBU SHOYU (SOY SAUCE WITH KOMBU)

Use for: a substitute for soy sauce, in fried rice, on raw tofu or with sashimi (tuna, salmon, sardines). Keeps for: 10 days.

MAKES 100 ML (3½ FL OZ) SAUCE

5 cm (2 in) square piece kombu
1 garlic clove, peeled but not crushed
100 ml (3½ fl oz) soy sauce

Simply infuse the kombu and garlic in the soy sauce.

Avoid serving this sauce with white fish, because the garlic overwhelms its subtle flavor.

PICKLING LIQUID

Use for: making quick pickles with about 400 g (14 oz) of vegetables. Keeps for: 10 days.

FOR 400 G (14 OZ) VEGETABLES

2½ tablespoons rice vinegar
2 tablespoons raw (demerara) sugar
2 tablespoons fish sauce
1 tablespoon salt

Combine all the ingredients in a small saucepan and bring to a boil on medium heat.

Put your choice of vegetables (cauliflower, carrot, cucumber…) in a resealable bag with the pickling liquid. Squeeze out the air and seal. Let the vegetables marinate for at least 1 hour.

You can add Sichuan pepper, ginger, pink peppercorns or any spices you like; you can also flavor the pickling liquid with 1 tablespoon of sesame oil.

CILANTRO SAUCE

Use for: perfect for dressing root vegetables (carrots, lotus root, baked sweet potatoes) or full-flavored red meats (leg of lamb, roast duck). Allow about 1 tablespoon sauce for 100 g (3½ oz) vegetables. Keeps for: 3 days.

FOR ROAST LAMB FOR 4 PEOPLE

½ bunch or 1 small bunch cilantro, finely chopped
1 shallot, finely chopped
1 garlic clove, finely chopped
2 teaspoons raw (demerara) sugar
4 tablespoons sunflower oil
60 ml (2 fl oz/¼ cup) soy sauce
juice of ½ lime

Place the cilantro, shallot and garlic in a metal bowl. Sprinkle in the sugar, without mixing it in. Heat the oil in a small saucepan until it starts to lightly smoke. Pour the oil into the bowl. Add the soy sauce and lime juice and combine.

This very aromatic sauce is a lovely green color and is quite unusual; it is my favorite.

SOY–BALSAMIC SAUCE

Use for: this makes a good base for a dressing for salad, vegetables and tofu, or can be used as a substitute for yakitori sauce (see p. 186).

TO DRESS
SALAD FOR 4 PEOPLE

3 tablespoons sesame oil
1½ tablespoons soy sauce
1½ tablespoons balsamic vinegar

Mix all the ingredients together. It is difficult to guess the ingredients in this sauce from its taste, as the soy sauce is slightly sweetened by the balsamic vinegar.

SHIODARE (SALT SAUCE)

Use for: perfect with roast chicken, tomatoes or a cucumber salad. Allow 2 tablespoons of sauce for 2 tomatoes. Keeps for: 2 days.

FOR ROAST CHICKEN TO SERVE 4

5 cm (2 in) leek (white part), finely chopped
2 cm (¾ in) ginger, finely chopped
60 ml (2 fl oz/¼ cup) first cold-pressed sesame oil
2 tablespoons coarse salt
1 tablespoon fish sauce
juice of 1 lemon
1 teaspoon cracked black pepper

Mix all the ingredients together.

RECIPE INDEX

INGREDIENTS INDEX

ADDRESS BOOK

NEZU—SENDAGI

This is the neighborhood I love to visit when I go back to Tokyo, between Nezu and Sendagi metro stations. There are small stores selling food, cakes and artisanal products, excellent Japanese restaurants, a very lovely Shinto temple, the Nezu Jinjya, and even a small onsen! You can spend a whole day there wandering at your leisure.

SOBA NOODLES

YOSHIBO RIN
2-36-1 NEZU
BUNKYO-KU, TOKYO
+81 3-3823-8454
11 am–3 pm and 5:30–8:30 pm
Closed Tuesdays

My, and my father's, favorite soba restaurant. The chef makes the soba noodles daily (see p. 50). It is pure pleasure to eat freshly made soba, delicious with a good glass of cold sake, just as Mr. Shotaro Ikenami, a true Tokyo writer, used to do.

CONFECTIONERY

KOISHIKAWA KINTARO AME
1-22-12 NEZU
BUNKYO-KU, TOKYO
10 am–6 pm
Closed Mondays

The famous Kintaro Ame candy store was founded in 1914, and is run by a couple of very sweet grandparents. The shop has always maintained the authentic taste of Tokyo confectionery (see p. 136).

TOFU

TOFU KOBO SUDA
2-19-11 NEZU
BUNKYO-KU, TOKYO

SHOPPING STREET

YANAKA GINZA SHOUTENGAI
3-13-1 YANAKA
TAITO-KU, TOKYO

This street holds all sorts of small authentic shops: the sake seller who offers you a tasting in the street; the fishmonger grilling eel; the shop that sells fresh, inexpensive vegetables... Although the shopkeepers don't really like people taking photos (especially without asking permission), mostly they are very friendly and proud of their profession. As you'll see, there are lots of people over 80 still working.

SENBEI CRACKERS

DAIKOKUYA
1-3-4 YANAKA
TAITO-KU, TOKYO
10:30 am–6:30 pm
Closed Thursdays

The best savory rice crackers in the neighborhood. The shop is tiny, but so pretty. If you are lucky, you might be there when they are grilling their senbei, one by one, on the charcoal barbecue. It is a beautiful sight, and the smell of the soy sauce as it caramelizes is absolutely irresistible (see p. 100).

A MODERN FISHMONGER

NEZU MATSUMOTO
1-26-5 NEZU
BUNKYO-KU, TOKYO
11 am–7 pm
Closed Sundays and public holidays

This is not a traditional Japanese fishmonger's shop. Minimalist and refined, everything is very clean and modern, and there is no unpleasant fishy smell. Every day, the owner selects only the best-quality fish at Tsukiji market. People in the neighborhood ask him to put together sashimi boxes for them, and they are as pretty as a box of jewelery (see p. 89). It is not cheap, but the quality is assured.

ASAKUSA

This is the area where you'll find theaters, temples and stores selling artisanal products, as well as restaurants serving the specialties of Tokyo cuisine. It is well worth wandering around the streets, visiting the shops full of kimonos and traditional crafts, seeing the oldest amusement park in Japan, and enjoying a meal.

ANGELUS

1-17-6 ASAKUSA
TAITO-KU, TOKYO
10 am–9 pm

An authentic café where you can enjoy yougashi, Western-inspired Japanese cakes, such as strawberry shortcake or roll cake. Their slowly infused iced coffee (Dutch coffee) is so good with their roll cake.

STARNET

1-3-9 HIGASHI KANDA
CHIYODA-KU, TOKYO
11 am–8 pm

This shop is in Bakurochō, not far from Asakusa. I go there to buy tableware (for this book, for example). On the first floor, you'll find ceramics from Tochigi Prefecture, known for its mashiko yaki pottery. On the second floor they sell clothes and accessories made from natural materials and dyes. They also have an affordable selection of pottery from young Mashiko designers. The shapes are very simple but original. I always come out of this shop carrying huge bags.

KAPPABASHI

KAPPABASHI DOUGUGAI

18-2 MATSUGAYA
TAITO-KU (the address of the
beginning of the street), TOKYO

Right next to Asakusa is a street
filled with shops dedicated to
cooking utensils (see p. 220)
and shokuhin sanpuru (the fake
plastic food displayed outside
restaurants, see p. 74). This is a
dangerous place for your wallet,
because you can find almost every
Japanese cooking utensil here,
including ones for baking, as well
as tableware. Allow half a day (or
more) to visit all of the shops. It is
very interesting and inexpensive.

TSUKIJI

TSUKIJI MARKET

5-2-1 TSUKIJI
CHUO-KU (the addtess at the
start of the market), TOKYO

The largest fish market in the world
(see p. 32). You can find everything
related to food and cooking here:
the best Japanese knife shops,
ultra-fresh fish, good restaurants
using fresh market produce...
The external market (Jyougai)
is available for tourists as soon
as it opens. The internal market
(Jyounai) is reserved for trade and
only open to individuals from 9 am.

If you want to enjoy sushi in the
market restaurants, make sure you
get there early, because by 7 am
there are already long lines.
Check the website for more detailed
and up-to-date information.

www.tsukiji-market.or.jp

HARAJUKU

YOYOGI PARK

2-1 YOYOGI, KAMIZONOCHÔ
SHIBUYA-KU, TOKYO

A large park close to the lively
modern neighborhoods of Harajuku,
Shibuya and Omotesando. It is next
to the Meiji Shrine, one of the finest
Shinto temples in Tokyo, where you
can watch a traditional marriage
ceremony. Families and friends
meet in this park to picnic and
people watch: you can see rockabilly
dancers and people dressed up
as dolls or cartoon characters,
an eclectic mix that is typical of
Tokyo. At the entrance there are
also yatai, mini Japanese snack
stands. And in springtime, the park
is packed with people who come to
see the blossoming cherry trees.

SHIBUYA

**The famous neighborhood of
modern Tokyo (the one on
postcards!) with neon lights, lots
of pedestrians, kawaii girls and
huge advertising screens, just like
you see in the movies.**

PARTYLAND

MARUHIDE BUILDING 2F,
13-4 UDAGAWA CHO
SHIIBUYA-KU, TOKYO

Japanese crêpes and frozen yogurt,
kawaii style. Just once, you might
like to try a Japanese crêpe: very
rich, very decorative and enormous
(see p. 124). This shop is in the
middle of Shibuya, where you can
find clothes and shoe stores,
fast-food restaurants and izakayas
popular with young people. It is
so much fun to see how lively and
colorful this district is: so many
people, so much noise, and so
many shops; it is almost surreal.

SHINJUKU

OMOIDE YOKOCHO

Just next to the Shinjuku metro
station (west "Nishiguchi" exit)
www.shinjuku-omoide.com

This the ideal place to make the most
of an evening exploring izakaya (see
p. 190). The choice of restaurants
and bars is enormous. Izakaya, sushi,
yakitori, ramen... Don't hesitate
to have one drink in one place,
another somewhere else... The bar
owners will offer you numerous
dishes to enjoy with a drink.

SUSHITATSU

1-2-7 NISHI SHINJUKU
SHINJUKU-KU, TOKYO

A very good Edo-style sushi
restaurant in the Omoide
Yokocho district, squeezed into
a very confined space (like other
restaurants in this area). Bear in
mind that sushi is served with salt
here, and a special sauce... not just
with soy sauce. The sushi chef likes
customers to follow his advice!
Wait before using soy sauce, and
try eating the sushi his way first.
You will discover the true flavor of
fish with the perfect seasoning.

THANK YOU

Thank you to Rose-Marie Di Domenico, my editor, who gave me the wonderful opportunity to create this book.

For the photos, thank you to Akiko and Pierre. And for the styling, Sabrina! It was so interesting to rediscover Tokyo with you. Akiko, you have given me so much inspiration, and your advice really helped me when I was stuck.

For Agatha, thank you very much for helping me, encouraging me, and correcting all of my French mistakes in the recipes!

Miyako, Yamato, Sabrina and Quintin, and my best friends Megumi and Marine, thank you for taking part in the photo shoots in Paris. I had lots of fun with you, and it gave me great pleasure to cook for you. Thank you, Ami, for your advice about cakes!

In Tokyo, thank you to Sam, Tomoko, Dai, Namazu, Jyun and Fumiya, for helping me during the trip. Thank you to all of the shopkeepers and restaurants that welcomed us with generosity and kindness, and inspired us. Thank you to Noriko and Mr. Wang from CHEF'S restaurant. You are still the best restaurant in the world and a source of inspiration for me.

And finally, a big thank you to my parents, who gave me the best cooking education. And thank you to my darling Hugo, for enjoying my cooking and sharing the pleasures of life with me.

First published by Hachette Livre (Marabout) in 2014.
Published by Murdoch Books in 2015, an imprint of Allen & Unwin.

English translation © Murdoch Books 2015

Photographers: Akiko Ida and Pierre Javelle
Styling: Maori Murota and Sabrina Fauda-Role
Graphic design and illustrations: Paris Playground
Editor: Alison Cowan
Translator: Melissa McMahon

HarperCollins books may be purchased for educational, business, or sales promotional use. For information please email the Special Markets Department at SPsales@harpercollins.com.

This edition published in 2015 by Harper Design
An Imprint of HarperCollinsPublishers
195 Broadway
New York, NY 10007
Tel: (212) 207-7000
Fax: (855) 746-6023
harperdesign@harpercollins.com
www.hc.com

Distributed throughout the world by
HarperCollins Publishers
195 Broadway
New York, NY 10007

ISBN 978-0-06-244668-8
Library of Congress Control Number 2015947086
Printed by 1010 Printing Group Limited, China.
First Printing, 2015

IMPORTANT: Those who might be at risk from the effects of salmonella poisoning (the elderly, pregnant women, young children and those suffering from immune deficiency diseases) should consult their doctor with any concerns about eating raw eggs.

OVEN GUIDE: You may find cooking times vary depending on the oven you are using. For fan-forced ovens, as a general rule, set the oven temperature to 20°C (35°F) lower than indicated in the recipe.

MEASURES GUIDE: We have used 20 ml (4 teaspoon) tablespoon measures. If you are using a 15 ml (3 teaspoon) tablespoon add an extra teaspoon of the ingredient for each tablespoon specified.